# HOW TO DEFEND YOURSELF IN THREE SECONDS (OR LESS)

**The Self Defense Secrets You NEED to Know!**

**PHIL PIERCE**

Copyright © 2020

# CONTENTS

# WHAT CAN YOU GET FROM THIS BOOK?

- **Do you know the 'trick' to talk your way out of any situation?**
- **How to unlock your brain's secret power?**
- **How can you win every single fight?**
- **The one easy body position to instantly improve your chances?**
- **Do you know the visual triggers that signal an incoming attack?**
- **Learn to train your brain to deal with panic**
- **Discover the 3 Second Rule**
- **How to fight...even when you can't see!**
- **How you defend against punches, kicks and more**
- **The killer 'mistake' with most people's favorite technique**
- **And much more!**

The simple aim of this book is to unlock your body's natural, powerful instincts and open your eyes to some of the little-known secrets of easy self-defense.

Clue: It's not like it is in the movies and nothing like you've seen in a martial arts class!

The techniques and methods within this guide are all designed to flow in the way your body wants to move and nothing requires hours of training or revision to understand.

This down-to-earth, no-nonsense approach has something for pro's and beginners alike!

*Ever wondered what it takes in a real-life or death situation to make the right choices? Or how to dominate any violent encounter on the streets? You may be surprised at the answers...*

## HOW TO USE THIS GUIDE THE RIGHT WAY (AND THE HALF-WRONG WAY...)

For many people, the temptation in picking up a book like this is to jump straight to the techniques in the latter half and start to figure out how to beat the living daylights out of the next person to give them any trouble.

Sure, you can do that, and the physical techniques alone offer a distinct advantage over someone with no knowledge, but without the surrounding understanding of the rest of this guide, you will only be getting about half of the picture.

In reality, self-defense is much more about preparation, awareness and using your brain, rather than your fists. Some people estimate only about 10% of self-defense is actually throwing techniques and while that may seem a little low, the principle is accurate.

Do the work upfront, gain the knowledge and understanding in advance, and you can master self-defense without even having to throw a punch.

In jumping straight to the techniques you can easily miss some very important elements and deprive yourself of something that could, when the chips are down, make all the difference, so take your time, look through all the parts and make sure you are prepared should the worst happen.

# DON'T END UP IN PRISON! (A FOREWORD)

Some of the techniques in this book are powerful. Lethally so.

As such, extreme caution should always be utilized when bringing any of the tips, tricks, and methods listed in this book.

By planning, being prepared and being smart you can usually avoid any conflict altogether, but if all that fails, and only then should you consider a physical response. Even then, given the chance to escape, this should be your first priority, not striking another individual.

However, when you truly do fear for your life and the conditions for a response have been met, you should respond hard and fast, overwhelming your attacker and breaking their momentum (a subject we will cover later).

To physically engage another individual with appropriate force, you must meet the following criteria:

- You have done your best to avoid the conflict.
- You have no option for escape or leaving the scene.
- You fear for your safety and/or the safety of those around you.

Only when all these conditions are met, should you jump into action. Even then, there is a very fine line between self-defense and becoming an attacker yourself and, as we explored elsewhere in this guide, the power of adrenaline clouds our judgment when things get hairy and it is at these times we are at the biggest risk of making a stupid decision.

Self-defense is always just that; defense.

We NEVER use these methods to attack beyond ensuring our own safety.

The laws around the world are different in every country and it would be difficult to detail the specifics for everyone but as a rule of thumb 'Appropriate Force' is the way to assess any situation.

Your physical actions to defend yourself should be appropriate to the threat you face and, if you have the chance to escape, you should always take it. Not just because it makes sense but because this is often a legal requirement.

In a court of law, defending one's person or property against a threat is usually permissible. Sticking around to inflict further damage, however, is not, and will land you in prison.

Always take a second and consider your actions, take a deep breath and choose wisely.

.   .   .

**Good:** You block an attacker, strike him in the face once and run away.

**Bad:** You block an attacker, strike him in the face repeatedly and kick him when he is down.

**Good:** You shake off an aggressor who grabs you, kick them low once and run away.

**Bad:** You shake off an aggressor who grabs you, kick them low once and run away then come back later with your friends and beat them to within an inch of their life.

Can you see the difference?

# FROM THE AUTHOR

Over the years I have trained in more martial arts and self-defense systems than I can count. I don't claim to have mastered them all, but I've seen a lot. Some have been traditional, some modern. Some have been very effective, some not just useless but downright dangerous!

Every violent encounter is different and while it's impossible to predict what will happen every time I have, in my younger years, been the victim of several violent incidents in which I was assaulted, mugged or just attacked for no reason, giving me a unique perspective.

Despite the negative implications of these incidents, it was the very same events that drove me into exploring the wonderful world of martial arts and self-defense. Now, with multiple instructor grades in different styles, years of teaching and training experience and a couple of Amazon bestsellers in my back catalog, I have managed to turn my experiences into something that can help other people learn about and protect themselves against violence in whatever form it takes.

Violence, it turns out, doesn't care about age, sex, who you are or your location and can rear its head any time. It is ugly, unpredictable and 90% of so-called 'martial arts training' counts for exactly nothing.

In today's unstable world of terror threats, school shootings and civil unrest, it's more important than ever to know how to look after yourself. The problem is that when adrenaline kicks in and our most primal instincts come into play we are, beneath it all, animals. Scrapping for our life.

This is embedded in thousands of years of our evolution so anything that runs counter to intuition is almost certain to go out of the window when things get real.

So those complicated blocks and twists, all those bizarre acronyms for remembering self-defense methods and all those technical martial arts classes will probably count for, at best 10% of what you do in a real life-or-death situation.

Repetitive drills perfecting these techniques can significantly improve that percentage but why fight against our instincts when nature has already wired us to protect ourselves anyway?

The aim of this guide is a no BS approach to self-defense utilizing deceptively simple techniques that build on your own instincts and make it easy to protect yourself against a threat.

There are no overly complicated techniques, no lengthy lectures and no tactics that should take longer than three seconds when used on the street. I hope you never need to use any of them, but if you do, you'll be glad you took the time to read.

Stay safe out there.


*- Phil Pierce*

# PART ONE

# UNDERSTANDING VIOLENCE

# THE 3-SECOND SECRET

The choice of '3 Second Self-defense' is not just for a snappy book title. It's not even just because three seconds looks good on the cover. The principle behind this guide is based on the fact that most violent events in life occur extremely fast and with little time for preparation.

Can you remember that last time violence threatened your life? Or can you remember the last time something sudden and stressful occurred? A car accident, an injury, a fight breaking out nearby? Anything?

Chances are you only remember snippets of the event and things were moving so fast you were largely acting on instinct. An instinct that kept you alive and kept you moving.

This is the core concept of '3-Second' self-defense

**In almost any violent encounter, the situation is resolved (for good or bad) in three seconds. Often even less.**

That's not to say fights or violent encounters don't last longer—they do, but remember we aren't talking about an organized bout wherein two opponents duke it out until one is the winner. We are trying to escape a threat and remove ourselves from danger—something that can and should be achieved much quicker.

There may be a chase or there may be a scuffle that lasts 10 minutes, maybe more, but the finishing technique, the one that stops the threat and gets you safely away usually happens in three seconds or less.

Later in this guide, we will explore a concept called the OODA loop; a decision-making process that happens incredibly fast and enables us to make strategic choices during high-stress environments. This includes:

1. Observing a threat.
2. Positioning to address the threat.
3. Deciding how to act.
4. Acting and observing that action.

It might seem like a lot is going on here, but the whole cycle happens incredibly fast, especially in violent encounters. This loop is also the same process an aggressor goes through and most of it will take place in the blink of an eye. If you can utilize techniques to break an opponent's momentum and strengthen your own decision-making process, you can resolve any conflict in seconds.

It's also worth noting that this doesn't always mean physical combat.

Within three seconds a potential aggressor can be turned away or defused through the correct use of body language or verbal cues, without even lifting a finger.

In fact, if we consider the implications of situational awareness and making yourself as difficult a target as possible it could be argued that three-second self-defense becomes zero-second self-defense. The fight was over before it started because you were never there, never chosen as a victim or slipped away unnoticed.

Whether you are a 20-year veteran of Martial arts or a complete beginner looking for tips on staying safe it's time to re-examine what we know about safety on the streets.

So while three seconds may seem a short amount of time it can be the most important few seconds of your life...

# BEAT BEING 'NORMAL'

When we talk about self-defense training, it is easy to get caught up in physical skills and strategies. While these are important, a psychological look at the normal response can be even more important in terms of being prepared to act. One specific psychological element of self-defense that you should become familiar with is something called the Normalcy Bias. You might also see it referred to as the "ostrich effect" or "analysis paralysis" (Hernandez, 2017). Let's explore what this is and why it is so important to be able to defend yourself swiftly and effectively.

**Your Instinctual Bias and Perceived Normalcy**

When psychologists talk about your "Normalcy Bias," they are talking about your predisposition towards certain thought patterns, generally related to emergency situations. Here are a few typical biases most people carry.

- They believe disasters are unlikely to occur.
- They underestimate the potential impact of an emergency situation.
- They believe life and society will always function in normal, established patterns.

- They don't think preparing for the worst is of value since the worst won't happen.

As you can see, the Normalcy Bias is a mindset that prevents people from preparing for a self-defense scenario. Though normal, it can cause people to be caught by surprise. Another danger is that people will find themselves in denial when something does happen. Because they think the worst is unlikely, they will be slow to react. When it comes to self-defense, this gives the assailant an upper hand because the victim doesn't start to run away or fight until it is far too late. The Normalcy Bias is the most common reason for a lack of training or preparation. It is also the reason most people freeze in the face of danger.

**Recognizing Imminent Threats**

Normalcy Bias doesn't just sabotage an individual's ability to prepare for and/or recognize a physical assault. Normalcy Bias may relate to any form of threat on a large or small scale. People who live outside regions with the highest risks of natural disasters such as tornados, hurricanes, earthquakes, or tsunamis might assume the risk is too minimal to warrant action. They fail to plan for fortifying their homes, sheltering in place, or evacuating. When people are caught off guard, they reduce their chances of survival and maximize the potential for loss, or damage to personal property. The same can be applied to smaller, more common disasters like house fires, car accidents, or personal attacks. Failure to recognize a potential threat or take any preparation steps is the equivalent of surrendering your ability to respond to that threat effectively.

**How the Normalcy Bias Affects Self-Defense**

Imagine you are out for a walk, minding your own business, and suddenly a threat appears. A perpetrator is coming towards you, shouting, fists raised. Your response could be one of three. You'll fight and protect yourself, you'll run and avoid the confrontation, or you'll freeze.

A lot of people freeze in this situation, even people with practiced self-defense skills. And the Normalcy Bias is often to blame.

A well-trained body can only move if the mind tells it to. Often the stress of the moment, paired with a lack of psychological mindset training, can confuse our brains. If you have never been attacked before, then it might be easy to assume it won't really happen. We convince ourselves that the situation isn't really a threat. The attacker can't possibly have any problem with you, maybe they'll stop and go away once they get a closer look. Maybe this isn't really happening at all. Your brain can trick you into thinking this is a normal situation that will be resolved peacefully. That's possible, but are you willing to risk your life over it?

Normalcy Bias can freeze your physical reaction and reduce your use of active awareness. The results aren't pretty. You only have a few seconds to decide how to react. If you don't, you may be injured, or worse. Though high-stress situations can be pretty powerful in overwhelming your brain with the Normalcy bias, there are some things you can do to prepare for it.

**How To Beat The Bias**

Mental training is the key to beating the bias. You can create new cognitive pathways—providing a familiar, predetermined reaction to dangerous stimuli. As previously mentioned, most people have a Normalcy Bias because they have never experienced a threat that caused actual harm, so they assume this one won't either. However, if you were attacked, you'd probably develop a different mindset pretty quickly. The next time similar conditions arose, you would be quick to fight or run to avoid a negative consequence.

The wonderful thing about the brain is that thinking and effective imagery can also condition a response. When your brain searches for a memory to reference, it doesn't matter if that situation was real or not (Reinhart, 2015). Training can be just as effective at the neurological level. When you think about a threat, imagining it clearly, your heart rate will start to rise just as if the threat were next to you. Use this to your advantage with the following visualization exercise.

1. Close your eyes.

2. Visualize a threat coming towards you. Use all of your senses to make the experience feel as real as possible.
3. See yourself reacting defensively, scanning the environment for clues, and preparing to run or fight.
4. Visualize yourself implementing specific self-defense techniques.
5. Continue your visualization until the threat is neutralized—either they have retreated, or they are immobilized in some way.

Use this exercise often. In fact, it's a good idea to spend some time visualizing after every physical training session, to solidify everything you have practiced. Hardwire your brain to associate a real threat with an effective response to beat the bias.

## Survival Psychology and Scenario Training

Psychologists believe that, during evolution, the Normalcy Bias was originally developed for survival. Animal predators are generally less likely to attack or hunt a still target. Moving creates more attention, causing the predator to focus and possibly even identify you as a threat. However, dealing with animals in the wild and humans in society is quite different. Humans aren't scouring the area for food or following simple, rational thought patterns. And odds are, you aren't hiding in a bush where the assailant might just pass by if you are still and quiet enough. Obviously, this freezing response won't help at all if a natural disaster is about to strike either. If you watch a huge wave approaching without moving, you are going to get hit hard and carried out to sea.

Though the evolutionarily developed freeze response can be powerful and paralyzing, you can train it away. Intense training places stress on your body and mind, pushing you to the edge where the stress response takes hold. There you are forced to choose between freezing and doing nothing, or running or fighting to protect yourself.

By applying realistic, scenario-specific training, you can mimic the sort of conditions that create this response, and you can experience the freeze that comes with the Normalcy Bias. When you are familiar with this response and can recognize it, you can reduce its power. You can train yourself to push through it quickly so your self-defense training can take over. This can mean the difference between freezing for three minutes or three seconds.

Prepare your mind to overcome the freeze in the same way you prepare your body to fight—through training. To review, you can train to beat the bias in three ways:

- Learning about the Normalcy Bias.
- Practicing imagery techniques to hardwire your brain to react.
- Using realistic scenario training to familiarize yourself with the freeze instinct and practice pushing through.

# THE BYSTANDER EFFECT AND WHY NO ONE WILL HELP YOU

Countless times we've read accounts of victims who have screamed for help, and yet no one has stepped in to save them. Catherine "Kitty" Genovese, being one of the most notorious examples. In 1964, at least 38 neighbors heard her being attacked and failed to intervene. If people see a victim in distress, why don't they take action? It is a question that has plagued psychologists for decades, and perhaps even longer.

After decades of study, the most likely explanation is something now known as the "The Bystander Effect". This bystander effect explains why no one bothered to move Marques Gaines out of the road after he'd been assaulted in 2016. It is also the most likely reason why dozens of teenagers stood around watching 16-year-old Khaseen Morris being stabbed in 2019. Why will no one help?

Let's look at how this phenomenon prevents good, upstanding people from helping someone in need. We'll also cover why this knowledge is an important component of your self-defense training and mindset.

## Defining "The Bystander Effect"

The bystander effect is also sometimes referred to as bystander apathy. Apathy being a lack of interest or concern. This sociopsychological response causes people to be less concerned and less likely to help when there are other persons present. Something about the existence of others changes our response. More than that, the bigger the crowd, the less likely it is that anyone will step up to the plate.

Studies show that when an individual is alone and witnesses someone else in trouble, there is a 75% chance that they will charge into action and defend the victim. Those are pretty good odds for the victim, but not a guarantee. This figure shrinks to just 30% if six or more people are present. And it falls lower as the number of witnesses rises. This phenomenon goes completely against our standard "safety in numbers" assumption. In this scenario, the victim is unlikely to be saved in a crowded place. But, why?

## The Psychology Behind the Phenomenon

When a bystander perceives a situation in which someone may be in danger, they actually go through five different cognitive processes. The result of these will determine their ultimate behavior—whether or not they will step in and help. The final action, or inaction, will depend on whether these five processes indicate the situation as being an immediate emergency for which they are responsible.

The decision is dependent upon this five-step process:

1. Observing someone in danger.
2. Interpreting the situation as an emergency.
3. Evaluating their degree of responsibility .
4. Determining which form of assistance is best.
5. Acting to help the victim.

This is the basic framework for determining whether to help. But actually, the decision can be a lot more complicated. A few more factors that can influence whether a bystander acts, including whether or not they *think* the victim deserves their help, the relationship between the bystander and victim, and the perceived relationship between the victim and the perpetrator.

It probably makes sense that people are more likely to help if they have some connection to the victim. Action is more likely if the victim is a friend, family member, coworker, or member of the same group.

Another big factor is whether the bystander feels strong or competent enough to help. Many people forgo helping because they don't know what to do or they aren't sure of their ability to carry through. The most frustrating part of this phenomenon is that people who defer this responsibility to a professional, aren't always motivated to obtain that help by calling 911 or flagging down a police officer. And while a paramedic might be needed, it really doesn't take a special skill to put pressure on a wound to help control the bleeding while help is on the way.

A bit of more promising information is that people are at least more likely to act in especially precarious situations. Active shooter situations and large structure fires invoke more bystander assistance than muggings or domestic violence. In this case, they quickly perceive that something is wrong and determine that action is needed right away. But why aren't they stepping in the rest of the time?

## Who's Watching Who?

One of the biggest factors that prevent bystanders from helping is ironically the presence of fellow bystanders. As previously mentioned, when an individual is alone, they are more likely to offer help. Conversely, there is a lower likelihood of helping if the bystanders consist of a group of people. Groups of bystanders who have no affiliation with one another—who are strangers—are extremely unlikely to help.

This is partly because people are hesitant to act against social norms. If no one else is acting, we presume that helping isn't acceptable. People in groups also tend to assume that someone more qualified will help. When everyone is looking to everyone else, no one ends up moving. No one takes responsibility for the victim.

The act of looking around to validate your decision is called "social proof." In an emergency, members of a crowd will look to one another for confirmation of the expected reaction. If most people are continuing on with their own business, then you become more likely to do the same. In modern society, blending in is more acceptable than standing out. And so, they choose not to act.

The truth is that people may use any number of reasons not to step in.

- They fear personal injury.
- They are complying with social norms.
- They feel incompetent or lack the skills or strength to help.
- They assume someone else will help and do so more effectively.
- No one else seems worried, so it may not be a real emergency.
- They fear the assailant.
- They are unsure of what to do.

However, there is one situation in which people in a group are likely to act. This is when people in the group have some sense of being a collective. Friends, coworkers, and classmates are more likely to help one another. This is true even devoid of a personal relationship. Simply being a member of the same class or seminar makes individuals feel responsible for each other and are thereby motivated to act. Why is this the exception and not the rule?

## Social Violence and The Bystander Effect

Social violence is broadly defined as any form of violence that has a social impact (Tremblay et al, 2012). This violence makes communities feel less safe. Examples might be gang violence, armed conflicts, segregation, or child abuse. When we hear about or see these things, they have an impact individually and socially. They affect not just our sense of safety, but also, the way we interact with one another.

Of all forms of attack, social violence shows some of the largest examples of the bystander effect. When certain types of violence become commonplace in our communities, we tend to look the other way more and more—to avoid being involved. We don't help.

With the advent of social media, there is another component that comes into play. More and more we see online videos of these types of confrontations in which the witness does not act yet records the scenario. Somehow, we have created a society in which people would rather make a video than use their phone to call for help. Inside these videos, we see other examples of the bystander effect as well. Often, we'll see people walking by, going about their day, without stepping in to assist the victim.

Help is right there, available, but it isn't stepping up. No one is being saved in these videos. These bystanders are not helping. They are all waiting for someone else to take responsibility and be the hero. And the victim suffers greatly.

Imagine if that victim were you? Or someone you loved?

## Applying "The Bystander Effect" to Self-defense

By now you might be starting to see that the Bystander Effect is closely related to self-defense. When people are being attacked, the Bystander Effect takes hold, preventing external help from taking action. The average citizen will not intervene, so it is important that you don't rely on them to. The only person you can rely on in these scenarios is you.

In order to protect yourself, you need to be ready to not only defend against harm but also to practice counter-violence. In most scenarios in your life, violence is not the answer. However, when your life is in danger, you need to be prepared to overwhelm and dominate the perpetrator, taking control of the situation. For this, you will need the right techniques, in addition to speed, power, and motivation.

The most important lesson you can gain from this chapter is to not let up just because a bystander comes on the scene. Too often, an individual will see a bystander or a crowd of bystanders, and they start to relax thinking, "I'm saved." This is dangerous.

If you ever feel threatened, don't expect that a crowded place will save you. Crowds may make an attacker less likely to continue the attack, but help probably won't be coming from anywhere, so keep your guard up and save yourself.

Expect that no one is even paying attention. Expect that even if a bystander does notice, they won't stop your attacker, and they may not even provide first aid afterward. Be ready to do it all on your own and be ready to fight tooth and nail if you have to.

# PART TWO

# UNDERSTANDING YOURSELF

# UNLOCK YOUR BRAIN'S SECRET POWER

## The 1,2,3 Approach

If you remember the start of this guide it said there would be no complex acronyms or pointless systems to remember in this book. This still holds true because the 1-2-3 approach isn't some manufactured system. It's actually what our bodies are programmed to do anyway. In a tight spot, this is what we have going on in our brain – whether we realize it or not.

The best techniques in a self-defense situation are always the ones that flow naturally and require the least mental effort. When the chips are down and stress is high, it becomes near impossible to recall technical, complex locks and blocks. This hesitation and confusion causes a delay in response and ultimately more risk for you. Still, many people train against instinct through martial arts classes, learning intricate moves that only work in very specific circumstances and often not under pressure.

Instead, the idea behind 1-2-3 is a combination of fight AND flight; our two most powerful instincts.

Boiled down to the simplest components 1-2-3 is essentially;

1. Avoiding the threat.
2. Counter-attacking the threat.
3. Escaping the situation.

That's it. I said it was simple!

## 1. Avoid the threat.

This doesn't just mean a block, pivot on the spot or fancy footwork, although the physical elements do come into it in the worst-case scenario. Avoidance also involves being prepared to avoid conflict in the first place, taking all the measures you can to stay safe and running away to evade an enemy before any violence occurs. This first phase is our priority in staying safe.

## 2. Counter Attacking

Counter attacking comes into play when avoidance has failed and we find yourself in a violent encounter we can't dodge. Assuming you are either unable to avoid the threat, or you have successfully blocked an initial attack, next is time to counter-attack hard and fast with a return strike of any kind. The aim is to break your aggressor's stride and reset their though process. In other words, making them think twice about proceeding.

## 3. Escaping

Never get drawn into a fight where you are trading techniques with an attacker. Your final priority after a successful counter-attack, or even one which gives you a split second of breathing space causing an opponent to stumble or fall, is to vacate the area and escape from danger as fast as possible. Check for other dangers before running away and getting to a safe place.

Escaping if you can is not only a top self-defense priority but a legal requirement in most cases.

Understanding this sequence is important, but it's not necessary to memorize the wording of this approach. The whole point is that we don't need to because the basics are already built-in. This page is just a reminder to let your body act how it should and build on your own instincts with positive actions.

Society makes most of us overthink everything on a daily basis and in an aggressive situation, this can be life-threatening. It's time to switch off the overthinker (your attacker obviously has!) and just act.

By focusing on 1,2,3; Avoid, Counter and Run, we remove any unnecessary thought from the process and enhance our built-in ability to protect ourselves and our loved ones.

# HOW TO WIN EVERY SINGLE FIGHT.
# EVER.

### *Fighting Fit*

What is the first thing you think of when considering self-defense in a dangerous situation?

Screaming Karate chops?
  Bruce Lee?
  An MMA match?

How about running away?
  It might not be your first thought but it probably should be.
  People define success in different ways and victory can mean different things depending on the situation, but too often the perception of a conflict, even on the street is that of a traditional fight where one contender beats the other into submission.
  So many of our values come from things we learned in childhood. The scraps in the schoolyard, the movies we saw and the TV heroes of the time. As such it's not hard to understand why people think '

winning' in any kind of violent situation involves teaching the other guy a lesson, or trading punches until someone is knocked out.

But when things kick off on the streets, this way of thinking is not only inaccurate but potentially very dangerous.

Remember,

1. There are no rules on the street.
2. There are no referees.
3. There are no points.
4. Anything goes.

Honor, sportsmanship and fair play are all creations of organized sports and none of these things are present when real unplanned violence arises. The only things that matter are your priorities for staying safe.

We are trying to protect ourselves and those we care about. By getting drawn into a conflict we are already starting down the path of failure for these goals.

In the chaotic world of sudden aggression or attack, the winner:

1. Survives the attack.
2. Prevents further attack.
3. Minimizes injury.
4. Goes home at the end of the day.

The truth is, in a violent and potentially life-threatening altercation, the 'winner' is always the one that gets to walks away. The one who goes home unscathed and gets to tell their friends about what just happened. Even if you don't end up fully unscathed and take a few cuts and bruises, if you escape with your life, you can be considered a winner in the battle.

So what is the easiest way to ensure this victory each and every time?

Don't be there.

## Victory through avoidance.

Avoidance is a massive cornerstone of self-defense and allows us a simple and effective way to ensure we meet the winning criteria for any altercation.

The easiest way to achieve this is to not be there, not get caught up in the altercation in the first place. If you have become swept into a dangerous situation though, escaping as quickly and safely as possible enables you to once again reach these goals.

You automatically win by not being a victim.

The ability to run away and protect ourselves from danger has saved more lives than any other single technique in history. It should be the absolute first line of defense in a threat situation and the second line if the initial threat couldn't be avoided.

In the animal kingdom two instincts battle for dominance in any given encounter with a predator. Fight or Flight. We will get to the fighting later, but as humans, we have developed an unnatural aversion to running away when a situation gets bad.

Normalcy bias plays a large role in preventing our natural instincts, something we will explore overcoming later. Then there is the afore-mentioned media. If we recall any of the latest batch of movies and TV shows, our hero almost never runs away, and if he/she does they almost always come back later to settle the score.

This is usually a monumentally stupid idea in real life but the concept that tough guys don't back down has been passed on through generations of storytelling and is thoroughly ingrained in modern society. So much so that today we think of running away as a cowardly dishonorable practice.

·  ·  ·

*Sure you may have had your face kicked in and lost half of your higher brain function but at least you stood your ground... You may struggle to stand it in the future however since your spine was irreparably damaged...*

The fact is that escaping from a situation is actually the single smartest move in any given self-defense situation. Be it before or after violence. Honor is a fluid concept and you should be far more concerned with being alive to later tell your friends about the incident than how tough you acted when it happened.

If you struggle to come to terms with this consider it a tactical retreat. A fight, not of fists, but of intellect. By choosing to escape on your terms you automatically gain the upper hand.

Most aggressors will not be bothered with chasing someone after they leave a scene. This is because the nature of your average aggressor is to attack an easy target. Once you require even a little effort they simply lose the motivation.

There are many ways to make yourself a more difficult target, most detailed elsewhere in this guide, but once the situation is escalating toward violence (or a threat situation is looking likely) escaping is usually the best way to diffuse it.

## How far and fast do I need to run?

.   .   .

There is no easy answer to this. Every incident is different.

As I mentioned most individual aggressors won't even chase you at all but a small amount might. This chance is increased if there is a group. This comes from a pack mentality. Again we can look to nature in watching how pack animals such as wolves and African wild dogs operate. Each member of the pack supports and pushes the next, escalating aggression and the chase.

Still, even wild animals know when a pursuit is a waste of energy and your attacker will too. Often immediately.

In any case, I would advise being able to clear an **absolute minimum** of **half a mile** if needed, away from the scene at an **average pace**. This gives you the opportunity to gain distance, seek cover or hide within a large radius.

Personally, I recommend being able to run a **full mile** at an average pace. We always err on the side of caution and this distance gives you a **comfortable advantage** over an untrained assailant. In a stressful situation, it's likely you will perform 30-50% less effectively than in training.

If you normally run a mile with little problems, that will become a half-mile under stress.

Many people then like to ask, what if my attacker is a marathon runner or a parkour expert? Yes, it's a possibility but it's incredibly unlikely and as such, we train for the median or most likely scenario, to be most effective.

Professional athletes are somewhat rare anyway, but those dedicated to sports and fitness are usually focused on just that and far less inclined to cause trouble in the first place. Much in the same way that practicing martial artists are actually far less likely to be caught in a fight because of their dedication to the morals and tenets of the style.

Even so, it's highly recommended to be fit enough to run half a mile at about 50% of your top speed.

This may sound like a lot but it really isn't. A short bike ride and a quick jog once a week will get you in shape quite quickly and even if these aren't your thing any cardio exercise that gets your heart rate going will help.

·   ·   ·

The big three of Cardio:

- Running
- Cycling
- Swimming

If you are interested in learning more techniques for improving combat fitness check out my other book; "Fitness Hacks: How to Cheat Your Way to a Better Body".

# HOW TO FIGHT BLIND

One of the worst situations to be in is when we lose the ability to see our opponent in a self-defense incident.

Of course, losing any one of our senses is a problem, but not being able to smell is unlikely to affect your ability to stay safe on the streets. In some places, it may even reduce distractions.

Losing or damaging our vision, however, is a major handicap if we need to protect ourselves. There are a number of ways it can happen; a strike to the eye, sweat, or most commonly, a strike to the nose causing the eyes to well up. (This actually works both ways so can be used to your advantage against an opponent).

People tend to panic when they lose vision and especially so when a threat is around them. However, this need not be the case when we realize that sight is only one of our many senses and losing it temporarily doesn't mean you are defenseless.

Firstly, protecting your face and head is of paramount importance, this is a point emphasized many times within this guide. A good guard with the hands up, palms open and body ready should be your default position.

When you are blinded though, your situational awareness will suffer. As such, you must turn to your other senses for an understanding of your surroundings.

**Smell:** Is there anything in the air indicating your location? Can you smell an opponent's aftershave or cologne? Can you smell cigarette smoke or marijuana?

**Taste:** Taken a hit? Can you taste blood? What about the remnants of alcohol or sugary drinks? Both could affect your performance.

While both of these have some limited use, Touch and Hearing really come into play once vision is obscured. With a little fine-tuning, you can enhance your ability to learn to trust these senses more and still defend yourself should your vision become compromised.

**Touch:** How does the ground feel? Solid or slippery? Scan the area, feeling out around you with one hand, while keeping the other to cover your head in a guard. Extend your hand and reach for the opponent or threat.

**TOP TIP: If you can touch something, you can hit it ... even if you can't see it.**

**Hearing:** Listen carefully for noises, sounds of footfalls or talking. Can you hear scuffing feet? This usually signifies sudden movement, which might require your reaction.

Any noise of cars or groups of people? Assuming you stay out of the road, a public place is typically safer.

**Exercise:**

1. Get a friend or partner and a focus mitt/pad. Ask them to hold it in place and strike it ten times with a punch off the rear hand. Pretty easy, right?
2. Next, the pad holder stays on the spot but moves the pad around as you try to hit it ten more times. A little more tricky but not too bad.
3. Now a challenge. Your partner continues moving the pad, but you close your eyes and try the same ten strikes. You might get lucky with a few glancing hits, but it will be almost impossible to land a good hit each time.
4. Finally, you use the sense of touch. For this last set, reach out with your front/lead hand and gently grab for the edge of the pad as it moves. As soon as you make contact, deliver that rear hand strike again. This time I guarantee you will hit it. The power of touch at work!
5. Release the grip and let the pad holder move it again, complete the reach, touch and strike drill with ten strikes on each hand before swapping to let your partner have a go.

The amazing thing is that even with no sight, we have an instinctive awareness of our own body, its reach, and its position. Think about it. If you close your eyes you can still touch a finger to your nose. We can, therefore, hit something we can't even see providing we can touch it with the other hand.

This guiding hand only needs a light contact for us to be able to engage our other hand, leg, knees or elbow, although a punch or Palm-Heel is easiest.

### Ready for a real challenge?

Complete the same exercise, with the pad striking and eyes closed but this time the pad holder moves away a few meters. When ready to begin, they call out to you a few times, guiding you to their location with voice only.

You then must use your hearing to position yourself correctly, shuffling forward each time with your hands up. When you make that contact with the fingertips, once again deliver the strike(s) to the pad.

The holder then moves away and resets to start again.

Give it a go.

# THE TRUTH ABOUT PANIC (AND HOW TO TRAIN FOR IT)

### *Training for Stress*

Adrenaline is a wonderful thing. It enables us to be alert and focused, it instantly wakes up the body in an unexpected situation and it can stimulate muscles beyond their normal capacity. Heck, adrenaline can even save lives when injected for allergic anaphylaxis. (As a peanut allergy sufferer this one is particularly appealing).

But Adrenaline also has a darker side. It throws your body into overdrive, pushing every system beyond its normal limits causing confusion, irrational behavior, and a massive come-down after the event.

In self-defense terms, Adrenaline gives us clarity and focus in a violent encounter and enables us to fight harder, run faster or last longer than usual...but at a cost.

Adrenaline also triggers panic. Panic is the dangerous by-product of the hyper-active mode our body goes through in a threat situation.

Panic clouds our judgment distorts our decisions and can make us act on pure emotion. This can be especially dangerous when we are angry or vengeful; feelings that could easily occur after an attack.

.   .   .

## So what can we do?

Everyone reacts in different ways to panic and addressing it is a personal experience, but there are a few methods for managing the surging stress of an adrenaline-fuelled situation.

The most common method for relaxation is deep breathing. The method I teach is based on a 4-4-4 count.

- Inhale for a mental count of four seconds.
- Hold for a count of four seconds.
- Exhale for a count of four seconds.

Repeating this sequence up to ten times is a proven method for slowing the heart rate and getting control of your breathing.

Also, be aware of your shoulders. Most people tense these under pressure and they rise up toward the head. Even with a good guarding block, you can relax the shoulders.

Finally, if you really want to give yourself an advantage under stress you can actually train for it.

## Training for panic

If you could train your mind to deal with panic it would be a big help, right?

Over the years, I have trained with a number of martial artists and self-defense experts who try to address this, but one coach who had himself featured on TV combining Chinese martial arts and self-defense taught a particularly impressive method for training 'panic.'

A technique I call the 'Panic Square'.

Quite simply, it is very hard to fool the body into reacting like it would in a real life-or-death situation. Somewhere, no matter how deep, our brain always knows when it is training. I.e. not really under threat.

The only way to get around this and induce real (controlled) panic is to take away the one thing it always needs; air.

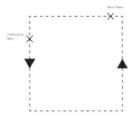

*IMPORTANT: Don't attempt the following exercise if you have any medical conditions or without supervision. This is just an explanation of a technique that worked for me; try it at your own risk. Don't be tempted to push yourself too far the first time you try it.*

To induce panic in a controlled way try the following exercise:

- Within a gym or large area work out a route around the outside, a square path of sorts.
- Set yourself a mark on the floor and start by walking around this route at a normal pace.
- After one lap, when you hit the start marker, hold your breath.
- Keep walking as before at the same pace.
- Eventually, you will start to feel desperate to breathe (panic sets in).
- Get to the point when you really need to take a breath.
- Take 5 more steps and raise an arm to signal this point.
- After the 5 steps breathe normally and relax.

During this last part, your body is experiencing panic, or as close to the real thing as you can get. The desperate need for air triggers the adrenaline and all the associated reactions with it.

If you can learn to control this sensation, relax your body and mind, focus on slowing your heart and understand that you are in control, you can eventually learn to better control the whole panic reaction.

The exercise can also be ramped up by jogging or even sparring for a short period while holding your breath, but remember to train ins short safe sessions.

This drill is quite intense. Always only try it if someone else is present and you are healthy. Don't do it until you pass out. This can cause long-term damage!

### Mask Training

For a slightly less intense, but also effective training technique, consider trying an elevation or altitude mask. These devices attach like a mini gas-mask around the mouth and nose and reduce the incoming oxygen content to force the body to work a little harder, simulating training at altitude.

While the evidence is mixed regarding their effectiveness for cardio-vascular pursuits and prices vary, these masks do offer a simulation of activity under some level of panic and can be invaluable. Regular practice with one can give you the mental tolerance to panic that is so hard to achieve under normal training circumstances.

View the range on Amazon at: **https://geni.us/trainingmasks**

# HOW TO BE BETTER PREPARED THAN 90% OF PEOPLE

The following are some considerations for general self-defense and awareness. Many of these are far beyond what anyone may need to undertake, and indeed we hope to never have to use them, but in being prepared for the worst-case we are able to easily deal with stations that aren't as severe.

Again, instead of trying to remember every aspect of these just try to understand the main point. Self-defense is, in essence, simple and we should take with us only the bare knowledge we need to survive. Anything else can confuse our natural, and often best, instincts.

## Awareness

### General Considerations

On the day you are attacked, will the weather be hot or cold? Will your assailant be large or small? Will there be more than one? Will they be strangers or people you know? Will they use weapons to assault you? Do you expect them to invade your home or vehicle? Or will you encounter a threat while walking someplace? Do you expect the attack to take place near pavement or on wet grass? Do you think that it will occur during daylight hours or after dark? Will it happen in the morning when you are full of strength and energy, or after a long and exhausting day at work?

Even individuals who train with the greatest dedication, and for the longest amount of time, will not be able to predict when and where they will need to use their training. It is important to be prepared for anything.

Still, there are a few things that you can always count on. The attack will happen quickly, and you will likely be caught off guard. There will be little time to think before you will need to defend yourself. The attack will be violent. It will not go as planned or follow the patterns used in your training. You will need to adapt quickly and without stopping to consider which techniques to utilize.

**Remember:**

- Avoid the initial attack where possible.
- Counter with your own attack and overwhelm the aggressor.
- Escape the scene.

### Environmental Considerations

In order to remain ready to defend yourself at any time, you should pay close attention to your environment. The weather often plays a significant role in your clothing choices. Consider the ways that those clothes could affect your mobility.

Your shoes may be especially important if you need to flee from an attacker. Do you typically wear tennis shoes, sandals, or high heels? Each of these options will affect your ability to run. What if you are barefoot when you are attacked? Would that hinder your movements?

Are you typically carrying an object such as a lunchbox, purse, briefcase, or backpack along your travels? Do you overload your arms with groceries? How would these objects affect your ability to defend yourself? Could they be used to your advantage in some way? Or do they make you more vulnerable to an attack?

. . .

## Ideally:

- Wear clothing that does not provoke others.
- Dress for the weather, but stay alert.
- Don't overload yourself with visible valuables.
- Dress in a way that allows you to move freely.

## Projection

Even before an attack occurs, it is possible to project your intent towards a potential assailant. This can occur inadvertently, and work against you.

However, you can also use this knowledge to purposefully send non-verbal messages to the people around you. You can control what you project. This projection does not have to be an honest portrayal of yourself, as long as it works to your advantage. There are many helpful strategies that involve misdirection or distraction. It is worth considering these techniques before they are needed.

## Projecting:

- Stand up tall and walk with confidence.
- Drop your shoulders and ease into a tall posture.
- Don't act like a victim and you are less likely to be one.
- But equally don't show aggression or anger, hold a neutral expression.

## Escalation

Similar, to your ability to utilize nonverbal communication, it is also possible to escalate a physical confrontation past the point of control. Every situation has the potential for various levels of aggression. Keep in mind; you may need to explain your actions to a law enforcement officer after everything is over. Whenever possible, it is best to defuse the situation as early as possible.

Passive body language and non-threatening behavior can go a long way toward neutralizing a situation. This guide is not focused on every detail of this (That will be included in a future book) but simple things like the open-hand guard (see later) will help a great deal.

Small misunderstandings, can get physical much too soon with the wrong verbal and body language. It is similarly possible, for a small scuffle to turn lethal in a matter of moments. Take advantage of any opportunity you get to diffuse the situation.

**De-Escalate:**

- Try to keep calm and you will keep the situation calm.
- Show open palms, not fists.
- Keep your voice even and steady.
- Breathe.

*Warning Signs*

Before a physical altercation, there are often signals which indicate that the aggressor intends to attack. Staying alert will aid you in noticing these valuable hints that danger may be imminent. These signs may also prove helpful when attempting to validate your actions before a court of law.

If your opponent exhibits tense shoulders, clenched teeth, a furrowed brow, narrowed eyes, or clenched fists then you may indeed be in physical danger.

This may sound obvious but such features can easily be overlooked when we are fatigued or distracted.

If an individual's skin begins to turn red, then this indicates that they are becoming angry or upset. A complexion that turns pale and/or white signals that their flight or fight response has been activated. This natural physiological event drains the blood away from the face, and towards the limbs to prepare for a fight or other physical action.

## Warning signs attackers may exhibit include:

- Redness in the face.
- Jaw clenching.
- The smell of alcohol.
- Repetition of words/phrases.
- Increasing volume
- Pack behavior (usually aggression/posturing around friends).

## Priorities

In every situation, your priorities will be different. You will need to become aware of these priorities in order to work towards the best outcome. If you are attacked within your own home your priorities might involve your loved ones or your personal property. In a mugging, attempted rape, or out-of-control argument, your priority might rest in protecting only yourself from harm.

Any event will carry its own variables, which will help you decide how you will act to eliminate the threat. It is best to consider your options through a process of internal dialogue before you find yourself in any of these situations. This will help you know how to respond without wasting time when there is little to spare.

Escaping the immediate danger should always be a top priority. Even if an attacker is in your home it is far better to escape and alert authorities than to risk life and limb for some valuables.

The only case wherein sticking around holds some importance is when other, more vulnerable people are involved. In this situation, the same principals of Block, Strike, Escape apply but you must try to strike with enough force to incapacitate an attacker and give yourself enough time to allow both you and the friend or family member to escape.

PART THREE

# HOW TO DEFEND YOURSELF

# 10 STEPS TO BETTER SELF-DEFENSE

The purpose of self-defense is to protect yourself and prevent injury. It is meant to keep you safe. When a violent or threatening situation arises, most of the rules cease to matter. You will need to do anything you can to counter the attack. Do everything in your power to secure a positive outcome. Sometimes "everything in your power" means brute force, sometimes it means running away. You may be able to use your trained techniques, or you may need to be more creative. Either way, there is one step that comes first—and that is taking steps to avoid the attack altogether.

While it is important to be able to defend yourself physically, it is even more important to be aware of your surroundings and make smart moves to avoid violence as much as possible. Sometimes this means staying away from dangerous areas. Sometimes this means keeping your eyes and ears open and paying attention. The sooner you detect a threat, the faster you can respond.

The best self-defense is always avoidance—putting space between yourself and the threat. De-escalation also has its place. Try to calm the situation, while also being ready to fight your way out. When you absolutely must, when there is no way to avoid a confrontation, be ready to use every tactic you have, and all of your power. Kick, bite, spit, gouge eyes, or pull hair. These moves aren't pretty or impressive but they often work when left with no resort.

In these stressful moments, where there is no other choice but to fight, there are ten core principles of self-defense that you can always lean on.

**Principal One:** Aiming for the weakest points.

While some humans are taller or stronger, they all have the same basic weak spots. Aiming for these spots gives you the most chance of causing pain and gaining the upper hand. Even the biggest, strongest opponent is not immune to punches, pokes, or jabs to sensitive areas. These include the eyes, throat, groin, and nose. These points are sensitive and lack the protective muscle that might cushion a blow to other areas. Direct your attack to the most vulnerable spots to make your opponent give up and back off. At the very least, the pain will distract them enough to throw off their own offensive and defensive strategies.

**Principal Two:** Responses should be fast and powerful.

Every second your response is delayed is another second for your assailant to gain the upper hand. Your reaction should be quick. This is where your training really starts to come into play. Express explosive power. Use your mind to focus all of your strength on effective blows. In order to work, your efforts must always be fast and powerful.

**Principal Three:** Speed and accuracy can trump strength.

While strength can definitely help in any self-defense situation, it isn't the only quality needed to protect yourself. Nor is it the most important trait to possess. What is more important? Having solid techniques that can be performed quickly and accurately. You can do without brawn if you are quick and efficient. With the right training and well-aimed aggression, a small woman can defend herself against a large, domineering man. Speed and accuracy can always trump strength.

When it comes to physical confrontation, the quickest fighter will always win. So, don't worry so much about any shortcomings in the height or strength department. These won't hold you back if you work on firing off a fast strike. Practice carefully and often to develop this speed as well as adeptness at assessing situations and making quick, accurate plans of action. Know what you will do if and when, and be ready. That's the key to defeating a stronger opponent.

**Principal Four:** Develop real-life skills.

Real-life isn't as controlled as the gym. People attack in different ways, not always expectedly. And they aren't likely the same size, height, or build as your sparring partner. Another variable is rage. Manufactured rage in a controlled environment can't always match the domineering effect of an individual who has been pushed to the brink of physical violence. And in real life, you won't always be able to see them coming; you could have to protect yourself in the dark without any preparation or you might find yourself backed into a corner with limited mobility.

Make sure your training emphasizes the ability to improvise in the face of actual real-life scenarios. In fact, if possible, you should over-train to the point of exhaustion. Develop skills to defend yourself when you are stressed and all your reserves have been spent. Learn all the basic techniques in ideal conditions, but continue to practice them in new ways, with new challenges. The more you do this, the better you will be equipped to protect yourself in actual, real-life situations.

**Principal Five:** There is power in repetition.

You will never master a skill if you only practice it once or twice. You might be able to mimic the motion, but this isn't enough. It takes repetition to hardwire the brain for quick, instinctual self-defense. This is the difference between surface-deep cognition and ingrained muscle memory. Elicit the power of repetition by practicing techniques over and over, in every possible scenario, until your body remembers faster than your brain can process the need for action. Repetition places important skills in the top drawer, where they are always ready for use. Don't leave your training rusting away in some dark and dusty closet. Keep practicing, all the time.

. . .

**Principal Six:** Keep it simple.

There is no shortage of so-called self-defense experts teaching showy, impressive techniques. While there is no real harm in learning some of these, one core principle will always prove true. Simple techniques will always be more effective. Don't overcomplicate your approach. When the stress of an attack kicks in, you don't want to find yourself struggling, trying to remember the right sequence of those five steps. Train the simplest, most effective approach so you can put all that wasted energy into fighting. Simple is always best.

**Principal Seven:** Adjust to your own strengths.

One of the most powerful and empowering core principles of self-defense is the idea that anyone can defend themselves. Sure, not everyone can perform perfectly executed kicks or punches or deliver earth-shattering power, but everyone can do something. Using your own strengths and abilities, adjust your approach to make the best of what you do have. Figure out what works for you and keep pushing through. If you are small, then you can be quick. If you are larger, you might not have speed, but you can develop power and learn to execute powerful punches. Work around your limitations and adjust to your strengths. Everyone can defend themselves in some way. Find the best way for you.

**Principal Eight:** Know when to stop.

Remember from the introduction to this chapter that the pure purpose of self-defense is to be able to protect yourself. The purpose is not to pummel, harm, paralyze, or kill your assailant. Use what means are necessary to protect yourself, but never more. Once you have established the upper hand and diffused the threat, it's time to stop. Maintain the self-control and discipline to be able to do so and then disengage.

**Principal Nine:** Maintain the higher ground.

As long as you stay on your feet, you can maintain a fighting chance. Once the fight moves to the ground, your options become severely limited and the odds of being overpowered grow exponentially. This is especially true if there is more than one assailant. Do everything you can to maintain balance and stay on your feet. While you should practice some limited ground-fighting self-defense skills, you should do everything in your power to avoid having to use them.

**Principal Ten:** Stay aware throughout the fight.

Mindfulness is important when it comes to avoiding a confrontation. When you are aware of threats in your environment, you can run away before it is too late. This is important, but mindfulness doesn't lose its potency once an attack is underway. Stay aware throughout the fight. You don't want to be surprised by a gun or the arrival of another assailant. Keep an eye on your opponent, their patterns or weaknesses, items in the environment you could use as weapons, and/or the right opportunity to escape. Stay aware of what is happening to improve your odds. Give yourself a fighting chance.

## Self-defense Training Never Ends

Self-defense isn't about exercising your ego or sticking with one specific technique. Remember, the primary goal is to survive. Whatever it takes to do that can be considered effective self-defense. Keep in mind that what worked yesterday may not work tomorrow. The dangers and situations are different every time. So, keep training and learning. You can never train too much or be too prepared.

# YOUR READY POSITION

*"If anything can go wrong it probably will go wrong at the worst possible time."* (*Murphy's Law*)

While this subject is covered in some detail in my other title: Self-Defense Made Simple and preparedness also includes training and preparation weeks and even months in advance, in this chapter we are going to briefly explore being prepared ahead of immediate violence by adopting a good physical and mental position. In other words, setting yourself up when the attacker is about to strike.

Being prepared involves two things:

- Ensuring we are in a position to protect our head, chest, and body as best we can.
- Ensuring we don't escalate the conflict.

We begin by assuming a non-escalating, "ready position" or guard. This is sometimes also referred to as the "head's up position". If you expect trouble, then you will need to do everything possible to prevent yourself from becoming an easy target. You never want to be caught looking downward, with your hands inside of your pockets.

Still, in many situations, it is important to prepare yourself without intensifying the reaction of a potential opponent. There is no need to yell and leap into an intimidating karate stance anytime you feel uneasy.

The ready position brings your hands out and up to the height of your chest, with arms slightly bent and palms toward the attacker.

This prepares you for any impending action, without creating a threatening posture and creates a physical and psychological barrier in front of you. Sometimes this barrier alone is enough to put off the casual attacker. Seeing your state of readiness and having to figure out how to get around your extended arms makes them lose interest.

## Balance

To establish good balance, assume a position with your feet spread shoulder-width apart, and with one foot placed in front of the other.

Angle your body slightly to minimize the target area presented towards your opponent.

Note how this type of positioning allows for fast movements. It also provides greater protection for your groin and solar plexus regions. This minimizes your risk of taking a direct hit from an opponent. It is essential, that you are able to maintain good balance, should you receive a blow or shove from an assailant. You will also want to be ready to move quickly to defend yourself.

## Considerations of Balance

- Inner Ear Mechanism: This mechanism is responsible for your body's equilibrium. It can be negatively affected by viruses, ear infections, and other physiological deficiencies.

- Physical Stabilizers: Your body uses its skeletal structure to maintain balance, and support your body weight. It also uses muscle control to help maintain balance while holding a stressful or awkward position.

- Sensory Perception: Visual and kinesthetic sensory feedback combine to paint a picture of spatial understanding. Together, these cues allow you to know which way is up. Sensory perception problems such as a knock to the head or on-going illness can lead to ailments such as vertigo or motion sickness.

## Breathing and Mindset

The way in which you act and how you breathe are closely related.

For one thing, your breathing can alert a perceptive assailant to your next move. This occurs through visible clues like your respiration rate, how fast you blink, and changes to the color of your skin. These clues can also broadcast the state of mind you may be in at any given time. You can use these kinds of signs to your advantage, by controlling them.

By demonstrating that you are not intimidated by an aggressor, you may discourage them from continuing their threatening behavior. The image projected towards your opponent can be a big factor in determining what will happen next. The other factor is the way you breathe. Breathing affects your current state of mind. This is why breath-work plays such a large role in the practice of meditation.

If you are breathing heavily, without having exerted a lot of energy, then it is likely a physiological symptom of stress.

The best option is to practice proper, deep breathing exercises which will provide greater control over the surge of adrenaline pumping through your body. It is also useful in preventing hyperventilation and other extreme reactions to stress.

## Psychological Preparation

Many theorize that about ninety percent of a confrontation occurs inside the minds of the participants. Yet, few individuals spend a similar proportion of their time training their minds for physical conflict.

Hence, it is necessary to reiterate how important it is to train your psyche in order to be fully prepared to defend yourself. You must ready your mind for any actions that the body may need to perform. Although we can never be fully prepared for the unexpected, taking a couple of seconds in advance to slow the breathing and plan an escape route gives you an immediate edge over the person acting without reason.

Even something as simple as reading this book starts to activate thought processes we don't normally use, which can be helpful should the worst happen.

Ultimately, however, training is the best tool for mental preparation. Weekly practice of self-defense, sparring or high-stress drills through personal training or something like Krav Maga can give you the necessary skills to handle sudden, unexpected threats.

·  ·  ·

## Verbalization

Voice is another powerful clue to someone's state of mind during a stressful event. Being able to speak in a confident and powerful manner is typically one of the first things to vanish when your body is under duress. Fortunately, you can train your vocalization abilities in order to maintain that confidence despite a stressful environment.

One way to do this is to practice speaking while hitting pads in a training environment and responding to mock attacks. These types of activities will teach your body how to maintain strong vocalization in the wake of an altercation.

- Try ten palm strikes on a focus pad.
- With each strike, give a strong command such as "Back off!" or "Stop!"

Of course, it's not all about martial arts training. Just the ability to project in public speaking will aid you in verbalizing your confidence. All of these skills can have a significant effect on an assailant. Pairing a sudden verbal command, with a physical strike can assist you in gaining the upper hand over an opponent. This technique takes full advantage of the small window of opportunity created by the shock attributed to the pain from a solid strike.

Another benefit of vocalization is the ability to sway the perception of onlookers. Vocalizing your stance can help these onlookers become aware of the justification behind your actions. The testament of these individuals may become invaluable should the need arise to justify your actions before a court of law.

E.g. Shouting "Stay Away!" or "Leave me alone!" will be seen far more favorably than the other guy cursing and threatening you.

Be aware that every confrontation contains three perspectives. These include your perspective, the opponent's perspective, and that of any innocent bystanders. Each of these can be vastly different. Communication can act as a bridge between your perspective, and that of a witness.

All three perspectives may be shared with a law enforcement officer, who will be responsible for determining whether you will be charged with a crime as a result of defending yourself physically. The way in which each perspective is communicated to that individual can drastically affect your perceived credibility.

## Being Assertive!

You will need to convey one important message to a potential assailant; **you are not an easy target**.

Part of not becoming a victim is knowing your rights in an encounter.

- No individual has the right to harm or threaten you.
- No individual has the right to steal from you.
- No individual has the right to make you feel endangered.
- No individual has the right to threaten your home or family.
- You do have the right to defend yourself if necessary and appropriate.

### *Identifying a Potential Threat*

By being aware of your surroundings and paying close attention to the individuals in your area, you may be able to pick up cues that an attack is imminent. There are also signs which can assist you in identifying the most dangerous types of assailants.

- Behavior: Is the individual acting in a way that makes them the center of attention? Do these actions make sense within the environment? Does anyone else seem uncomfortable? Are they looking you in the eye or avoiding contact?

- Hand Position: Where are the individual's hands located?
  Are they holding anything which may be used as a weapon?

- Posture: Is the potential assailant standing near a doorway to
  block your escape? Are they limiting your movements or
  trying to surround you? Do they seem tense or relaxed?
  Based on the postures of other individuals in the area, does it
  seem as though anyone else is acting with them?

You can turn the same close attention to yourself. Consider what kind of vibe you are giving off and whether you might be exacerbating the situation. This skill will be particularly important if you come into conflict with an individual who is emotionally disturbed, or a police officer who might misinterpret your intentions.

**Response to the Threat**

The legal definition of a threat is a perception that your life or well-being, or that of someone near you, is in imminent danger. Taking this definition into consideration, you will need to be able to communicate a reasonable justification for your deeds. Your explanation will need to answer several questions, including those in the list below. Establishing a justification may be necessary to demonstrate to a court of law that your actions were appropriate and necessary.

1. Could you have found a way to escape?
2. Were you in real danger?
3. Does your attacker still pose a threat to your safety?
4. Would another rational individual have responded in the same manner, if they faced the same circumstances?
5. In what way did the attacker make you feel endangered?

## Ready-Position Priorities:

1. First, protect your brain. Strikes to your head will slow you down or take you out of the game altogether.
2. Keep your hands up and ready for action, but do not escalate the situation. Be sure to lift your arms in a manner that cannot be interpreted as threatening.
3. Utilize body language cues. Keep your eyes facing forward, your shoulders back, and your feet spread apart. Eye contact can intimidate your attacker.
4. Do everything you can to avoid a physical altercation. Demonstrate that you do not wish to fight. Show any potential witnesses that you are not the instigator of the situation. An important part of self-defense is legal defense after an altercation occurs.
5. Use vocalization tools in an attempt to avoid a physical altercation. Make an effort to avoid your assailant with phrases such as: "Calm down.", "Stay away! Get back!" or "Leave me alone, I don't want to hurt you!"
6. If you are attacked you will need to act swiftly to protect yourself so don't hesitate. But, you will also need to stop just as swiftly when the aggression has ended. You MUST stop too.

# ESSENTIAL TOOLS

*If you are interested in regular training for self-defense there are generally three categories in which to practice*

- Techniques: involve learning proper forms, positions, and technical variables within a potential confrontation.

- Exercises: are the activities used to develop an individual's skills and to increase their overall performance.

- Drills: gradually combine qualities like awareness, rhythm, and timing to acquire the psychological mindset required for a successful defense.

**Hand Strikes:**

Most people automatically think of punches when it comes to a fight. But here's the bad news; if you hit someone with a full-strength clenched fist punch there is an excellent chance you will break some fingers.

Punches work well against soft areas like the stomach or even throat but if you accidentally hit someone on the forehead you can forget using your fingers again for the rest of the night.

Consider instead the palm-heel-strike as your go-to default technique. (See later) Other upper-body strikes include:

- Claw hand
- Elbow
- Hammer Fist
- Finger Jab
- Thumb Gouge

*A simple palm heel strike*

*A simple straight punch (vertical fist)*

## Kicks:

Don't go high with your kicks. Keep them low and aim to either push an opponent away or strike a sensitive area to incapacitate them (Knee, Groin, etc).

- *Front/Thrust Kick*
- *Heel stamp*
- *Snap/Toe strike*
- *Side Kick*
- *Round Kick*

*A simple shin kick*

## Targets:

Target zones are sensitive or special areas to aim for in neutralizing an attacker's mobility. Most of us know the groin is especially susceptible on men but also consider:

- *Ears/Eardrums*
- *Throat*
- *Jaw*
- *Eyes*
- *Nose*
- *Solar Plexus (Center of the chest)*
- *Knees/Elbows*
- *Fingers*
- *Toes*

*Elbow Strike to Jaw*

# USING DISTRACTION AND EVASION

Never underestimate the power of Distraction to diffuse a situation or Evasion to avoid further conflict. Both tools usually allow the prevention of violence, or further violence without even throwing a strike of any kind.

## Distraction

The basic principle of distraction is a deflection of aggression away from yourself. Many would think of this in the physical aspects of self-defense, i.e. physically doing something, but it also refers to the spoken tricks you can use to throw off an attacker.

In fact, some of the most inventive and effective uses of distraction occur in the earlier verbal phase of a conflict.

## Physical Distraction

Physical distraction works by using some motion or movement to attract the eyes of an attacker one way, while you move in another. It uses the same principles of misdirection that a magician might use, but instead of trying to dazzle an audience, your distraction is designed to give you a split second of safety, where you can either strike or make your escape, (or both).

Remember, once violence is imminent, your attacker might be expecting you to throw a punch in retaliation since this is an expected response.

What they won't expect is an unusual counter attack coming from another direction.

- Throw keys or credit cards at an attacker's face, then run.
- Toss your cash or wallet to the side to distract a mugger, as you reach for a weapon.
- A drink thrown toward an aggressor's eyes.
- A low kick to their knee, to distract a strike to the face, before escaping the scene.

Physical Distraction tips:

1. Aiming for the eyes is an excellent target, since this is one of the most vulnerable parts of a person, and causes instinctive flinching.
2. Similarly, lots of small items thrown work better than one large item, since they are harder to register and block. Even better, consider using a liquid or spray.
3. Distraction should be fast and followed up by decisive action. You probably won't get a second chance once your opponent wises up to your techniques.

One important thing to remember is that a physical distraction needs to draw attention away from you and what you are doing, not draw more attention to it. So, try to keep the target zones away from your head and upper body.

· · ·

## Verbal Distraction

When violence is imminent there will usually be an escalation through shouting or aggressive talk. Your attacker will be building their own levels of aggression in this phase and the whole thing will be directed at you.

Facing it head-on with your own shouting and addressing what they are actually saying usually just leads to more aggression. The attacker is filled with adrenaline and nothing is going to stop that.

But what if we could redirect it?

Deflection is a powerful verbal distraction tool you can often use to bounce aggression off in a different direction and completely throw your opponent off their game.

The concept is simple when the aggressor starts shouting and getting in your face, you pose them a completely unrelated (and non-aggressive question). The more random and confusing the better. This calls a halt to their rising anger and spins their train of thought off in an unusual direction. It also causes a brief short circuit in the aggression cycle, forcing them to re-assess what is going on.

This moment of confusion causes a large adrenaline crash, where the previous elevated levels are now dropping. After all, it's hard to be angry if you have no idea what is going on. This period of distraction is when you make your exit.


E.G

An aggressor might ask:


"WHAT ARE YOU LOOKING AT?!"
"DO YOU WANT A FIGHT?!"
"YOU THINK YOU'RE BETTER THAN ME?!"


These kinds of questions have no correct answer. Instead, redirect them with deflection.

·   ·   ·

"Did you see that purple car?"
    "Do you know what time the last train is?"
    "Have you ever been to Burkina Faso?"
    "When does it get dark around here?"
    Etc.

Anything off-the-wall and unexpected works. The weirder the better, so long as it makes them think.

Suddenly, the opponent is off-guard and you have an opening to escape. (Not to stick around or escalate the situation).

This is a technique that has been popularized across martial arts and self-defense systems in the last few years, largely thanks to self-defense coach Geoff Thompson. Look into his guide to 'The Fence' for more.

As a final proviso, remember that many aggressors and muggers may also try to utilize some simplistic methods of distraction, especially in the opening stages of approaching you. Try to keep your eyes open and if a situation feels bad, make your escape quickly.

## Evasion

The importance of running away has already been discussed in this book, but evasion is just as important as a distraction and if you find yourself facing sudden violence, getting away might just save your skin.

If an attacker or group gives chase there a few steps you can take to minimize the chances they will find you.

**Shape** – At a quick snapshot we can recognize the form of someone. If they run we are looking to find that shape we have already registered. By adding or removing headwear, changing or discarding a coat or bag you can change the way you appear at a glance.

**Color** – Similarly we can establish color and patterns easily after a quick look. In an evasion situation, you can discard clothing to change how you look. Don't get hung up on specific details. The best approach is to go from light to dark or vice versa as this is the quickest method of recognition.

**Blending** – A pursuer will be looking for someone on their own. If you can blend in with a crowd, pretend to be someone in a coffee queue or a group of passing friends odds are you will be much more easily overlooked.

**Movement.** – In a high-stress scenario, most people will move in an erratic and panicked manner. If you can gain some distance, utilize the other tips and then move in a slow, controlled way like a normal pedestrian, chances are you will be blend in more easily with other people on the street.

# HOW TO BREAK YOUR OPPONENT'S LOOP

If you spend any length of time exploring self-defense or specific styles like Krav Maga you might hear references to the OODA loop being used. But what is it and how can you use it quickly neutralize an opponent and control the situation?

While it might sound like some kind of exotic martial arts technique the OODA loop is actually a term coined way back during the Vietnam war as a military strategy for handling and understanding a combatants thinking.

Originally developed by US Air Force strategist Lt Col. John Boyd, the idea of the OODA loop was quickly introduced as a tactical concept for air to air contact between fighter jets. Since then it has been adapted for use in multiple branches of the military, sports, business and of course, self-defense.

OODA stands for Observe, Orient, Decide and Act. In essence, it is a simplified breakdown of the way our brain makes decisions, and it applies to everyone, both aggressor and potential victim. It's known as a loop because the process feeds back into itself with each step, pushing the next ahead and always in the same order, like a spinning wheel.

The interesting aspect of the OODA loop is that knowledge of how it works makes it much easier to break an opponent's loop and force them back to the start, effectively breaking any attack and putting them on the back foot.

## The OODA Loop steps from an attacker's POV

- **Observe**
- The attacker observes (sees) someone they can make into a target.
- **Orient**
- The attacker orients (positions) themselves ready to inflict violence.
- **Decide**
- The attacker decides to throw a right haymaker straight toward the victim's face.
- **Act**
- The attacker carries out the decision by acting. They swing for the person they targeted.

Feeding back into the loop, the attacker then observes (Step 1) how effective their actions were and continues to press the advantage.

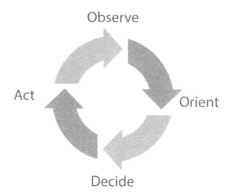

The good news is that by interrupting this loop at any of the four points, you start to break down an aggressor's decision making process, giving you not only time but also the upper hand in a violent encounter. The bad news; chances are you might only be at step one yourself (observation) when your opponent is already at step three or four, close to taking a swing at you.

Ultimately, the further along an attacker is in their process, the harder and faster you must respond. For example, if violence is about to happen and someone swings for your head, block with your own arm and strike them with a palm heel to the face with power. Nothing breaks a thought process like a strike to the face. Not expecting the counter-attack and block, the opponent is forced to rethink the situation, restarting the loop and giving you escape time.

Let's take a look at that sequence again, but instead, using strategies to break down an attacker's loop.

## Observe

By making yourself harder to see, unremarkable or by using the environment, the aggressor cannot start the loop against you.

## Orient

Place yourself out of harm's way, become impossible to touch or evade the attacker altogether and the loop breaks down.

## Decide

Overwhelm an attacker with counter-attacks and a loud assertive voice (go loud). Force them to keep rethinking the situation and the loop cannot continue.

## Act

Block, move, strike and use brief aggression. Stop the attacker acting, neutralize the threat and escape.

·  ·  ·

Ultimately aim to give yourself the best chance at breaking an opponent's loop by catching them early in it. If that doesn't happen, make any block and counter-attack akin to a controlled explosion and you can almost completely break down their thinking process.

Be unrelenting, explosive and overwhelming. Then escape.

# GRAPPLING IN SELF-DEFENSE

## *Going to Ground*

Many people are familiar with the stand-up and striking styles found in numerous martial arts but grappling forms like Brazilian Jujitsu, wrestling, Sambo and many more are also fantastic styles with a number of benefits, which begs the question; why are there no ground fighting techniques in this guide?

After all, if you watch any MMA match, street-fight or even a schoolyard scuffle, most people end up rolling around on the floor before the scrap is over. Surely it would come in handy to know this stuff?

A considerable amount of research went into this book and after consulting with top martial artists and personal protection experts, it became clear that ground fighting (grappling) is generally NOT recommended for a self-defense situation.

The surprising truth is that while grappling styles have an immense amount of value, especially in a one-on-one 'fight' scenario, they aren't ideal for looking after yourself on the street simply because we are actively trying to avoid getting caught in a fight situation.

The longer you are engaged with an opponent the more risk you face. The more risk you face, the less chance of successful self-defense.

That's not to say you should give up on any ideas of learning grappling styles. You will certainly develop some important skills if you pursue one, but for pure self-defense purposes, grappling is risky for two major reasons:

## 1. We don't know what the ground will be like.

We can't control when we will need to use self-defense skills. It could be at home, on the street, in a grass-covered park, or in a run-down dive-bar. The bottom line, we have no idea what surface we will be dealing with.

If the floor is covered with glass (as in many nightclubs), rocks, concrete obstructions or sharp steps, the last thing you want is to be throwing yourself on it. Let your enemy suffer the consequences of a tumble on these surfaces. Stay on your feet if you can.

## 2. We don't know how many people we will have to engage.

Similarly, we can't control just how many enemies we will have to defend against. If you are taking on an aggressive group of drunk youths, it doesn't matter if you are a Gracie master of Brazilian Jujitsu. Rolling around on the floor and locking yourself into an arm-bar with one of them leaves you dangerously exposed to the rest. All it takes is a sharp kick from someone to your ribs, to end up having a very bad day.

Not to mention the danger of being at a height disadvantage to all around you.

. . .

There are some limited cases where good grappling skills will come in useful on the street. If conditions all line up you may be at an advantage but these are rare and remember this guide is all about 3 Seconds. If you can't get in, get out and run it's probably not much use to you.

## Recommendations

If you'd like to learn more (and I still recommend them for fitness and technique) look into the following:

- Brazillian Jujitsu
- Traditional Jujitsu
- Judo
- Sambo
- Wrestling

While getting into a grappling situation is a bad idea, it is worthwhile knowing what to do if you find yourself taking a fall...

# HOW TO FALL SAFELY

It may sound odd but falling correctly is quite an art form. In a real-life self-defense situation, you don't really want to be on the ground for long for many reasons we've already covered. But, if you do find yourself taking a tumble, landing correctly can make the difference between being able to quickly get back up or face-planting and taking yourself out of the fight.

## The Break-Fall

The break-fall is a technique practiced in a variety of martial arts including types of Judo and Jujitsu. The basic principle is that you shape your body to reduce the damage taken when you hit the ground and spread the impact across a larger surface area.

You can investigate the details of this technique in any of the numerous videos online but in essence, you are aiming to lightly strike the ground with the flat of your palms as your backside and lower back hit the deck while tucking the head in to stop it impacting the floor.

## Rear break-fall

1. You know you are going down, accept it and prepare to act.
2. Start to fold your body down, bending at the knees and waist. Lower yourself down and assume control of the descent.
3. Tuck your chin into your chest to prevent your head from hitting the floor.
4. As the majority of your body hits the ground, slap your palms firmly (but not forcefully) into the ground to spread the impact. The force used depends on how hard the surface is.
5. Breathe out. Try to breathe naturally and exhale as you impact to reduce body tension.
6. If falling from some height, carry the motion into a roll in the natural direction the body is moving.
7. Come to a stop – and get up, quickly!

*Spread your impact when landing on the floor.*

**Front break-fall**

1. As you start to fall forward, bend the knees to reduce the fall height if possible.
2. Bring your arms up, hands protecting your face (this should be fairly instinctive anyway) and make a triangle shape with the hands and forearms to reduce any impact on the wrists.
3. Turn the head to the side (to avoid impacting with your face, in case the break-fall fails)
4. Land with the knees (or feet), hands and forearms making

contact with the ground similar to a plank position. The aim is to reduce the whole body hitting the concrete.

5. If a slow fall is occurring, you can use a push-up style technique to get back up quickly.

## Side break-fall

1. Again, if time allows, bend the knees to reduce fall height. Some styles advocate kicking away the inside leg, but you may not have a chance.
2. Engage the head and tuck the chin, to prevent any head impact.
3. Push the inside (falling) arm forward at eyeline with palm down.
4. Roll the body to the ground, impacting along the falling leg and flat part of the falling shoulder.
5. Slap the ground lightly with the falling arm and hand. (The harder the surface, the more gentle you need to be with this).
6. Get back to your feet as quick as possible.

Side and forward break-falls follow the same principles of lowering the body as much as possible to assume control of the drop, then while keeping control of the head, slap the hand(s) into the ground to absorb some of the impact.

Find a soft surface (ideally a training mat) and practice dropping your weight with as much control and safety as possible. Ready to take it further? Search break-fall videos online and give some a practice yourself. You don't need to reach the heights of a Judo master, but learning how to reduce the impact can make a big difference if you do take a tumble.

Break-falls are designed to reduce pain and injury, not cause it. If you find it hurting, try it on a lower or softer surface until it gets easier and/or your technique improves.

# HOW TO PROTECT YOURSELF ON THE GROUND

If you do find yourself in the unfortunate position of being on the ground with the threat of an attacker still on their feet it's important not to just curl up in a ball and expect a kicking. Doing this just makes you an easy target.

You still have a number of options and, while you are at a disadvantage and should get up as quickly as possible, you aren't down and out yet!

If we consider the change in dynamic for a moment, all that has shifted is the height at which a conflict can now take place. You still (hopefully) have all your limbs available to protect yourself while the attacker can't feasibly use their arms without bending down to your level. Of course, the attacker's mobility will now be far greater than yours and they can move with much more ease than you.

You both have certain advantages and certain disadvantages if one takes a fall and as such you enter a kind of stalemate.

It's important to note, however, if you do land awkwardly, try to roll onto your back as quickly as possible to free up the use of your limbs and raise a guard of some sort.

1. In the very first instance when you find yourself on the ground, protect your head. (Remember, this is the light switch for the body!) Put your hands up to either side of your head (Like you are cupping your ears), with elbows pointing forwards covering the sides of your chest. This step is to minimize any attack that may occur quickly after they see you go down.
2. Bend the knees. This again protects access to your torso and sensitive organs, creating a barrier with your limbs.
3. Use one or both soles of your feet facing your opponent.
4. Assess your situation. If the threat is to the side try to spin to face them so you can utilize your legs for kicking and see what is happening.

*Protect all the important parts of your body while exposed on the ground.*

## Striking Back

Make sure you are still seen as a danger to the attacker even while you are on the ground. Unless they are extremely determined, most aggressors are simply opportunists and the moment you become too much hassle they will give up and leave.

Your ability to strike with your hands will be minimal so your legs become the go-to technique.

Try to imagine a cornered snake here. This is your approach while grounded.

You are lower and perhaps smaller than the threat but you can still lash out with a quick and painful strike if needed, keeping the attacker wary.

The simplest and most natural strike from this position is a thrust-type kick.

With the attacker in front of you bring one foot up ready to snap a kick out quickly and aim low – for their shin or knee. (Try not to aim higher; it may throw you off balance).

If they are slightly further away and your upper body is at less risk you can plant both hands on the ground, raise your backside and snap a kick out further. This can often catch them off guard and even if this doesn't connect it can offer a vital few seconds distraction as they recoil out of the way, giving you a chance to get up.

Don't worry too much about the type of kick in this situation, just aim to hit hard with the heel or sole of the foot. The technique is less important than being quick, powerful and creating space for yourself.

*Snap a kick at an opponent's knee or shin to give yourself space.*

### If they try to get on top of you...

If an attacker evades your kicks and tries to physically get on top of you, to either inflict more damage through punches, or god forbid attempting some form of sexual assault, it's time to utilize the stronger muscles in your legs.

Many grappling Martial arts use a simple concept of a 'guard' while on the ground. There are numerous types but the main principle is of controlling an attacker's body while on the floor. In the spirit of simplicity, we want the most natural and effective forms. There is no need for technical names or martial arts styles here.

. . .

**In the case you notice your opponent is just trying to get on top of you;**

Use your legs!

With your back to the floor, quickly bring up one or both feet and the soles to face the attacker with your knees bent. If they still close in use the strength of both legs to push them away with your feet and ideally kick to the groin or knees. Remember to keep your hands ready to protect your head and upper body.

**If they are already close, between your legs or leaning over you;**

You can use hand strikes to keep them at some distance but here you need to free up at least one leg to utilize its power. If you find you don't have much movement with your legs try rocking slightly from side to side.

Wedge a knee between their arms and chest, creating space and potentially using it as leverage. Bring up a foot and plant the sole on their hip bone then push hard and fast. This pivot point should change the balance position.

If they are close enough to use their hands, odds are you can use yours too. If possible remember the palm-strikes from earlier. Or go for a simple eye gouge. (There are no rules here!)

**Top Tip. The underside of the nose is also incredibly sensitive. Even a light push here can dissuade someone.**

Remember this isn't UFC. Get them off you, get up and escape. Don't try for any complicated locks or submissions.

Now you've managed to get the attacker to back away with a kick or perhaps you've spotted a gap, it's time to get up. The right way...

# HOW TO GET BACK UP

**"Duh" – I hear you say. "Just put your feet down and get up!"**

While this approach works for your average toddler taking a tumble, on the street simply planting your hands down and getting to your feet causes a big problem in that it ties up the majority of your limbs in the motion.

Think about how you would normally get up off the floor. One or both hands push you up and your feet tuck underneath to bring you upright.

In this scenario you have nothing left to guard yourself should an attacker make a move.

If you have a significant distance over an attacker, this might work, but it's better to be cautious .

Instead, we want to allow at least one leg or one arm the freedom to protect our face or important parts as we get up. This is an approach sometimes advocated by styles such as Krav Maga where you may have to fight your way back up from a disadvantaged potion.

1. From your defensive floor position pick a moment when you see a chance to get up (A moment when your attacker is distracted, off-guard or pushed back by your kicks).
2. Lift one leg ready to kick out forward, giving yourself space to get up.
3. Lift the opposite hand to cover your head as you ascend.
4. Make the kick if needed and as you bring it back in tuck it under your body.
5. Use this leg to now push to your feet, all the while covering your head and face with the free arm.
6. Get back on your feet as quickly as possible.

*The hand guards the face, the kick pushes an opponent away then tucks back underneath to push you to your feet.*

*Tuck the feet back beneath you to get up.*

Note: If you are not confident in your balance you can leave either both feet or both hands on the ground but make sure one or the other makes a move to protect yourself!

# YOUR SELF-DEFENSE GOALS

When working out what techniques to use in a situation it is often best to think of what you want to achieve from the scenario before using any movements take place. Trying to do this when the adrenaline is pumping becomes near impossible, so take a notepad and think now in advance about the kind of things you want/need to achieve if you were attacked.

Of course not ending up injured is an obvious goal for most people, but beyond this, you can analyze how things would play out in an ideal situation. For example, self-protection goals can usually be broken down into 3 tiers; Essential, Important and Optional.

**Essential goals** are just that; the overall crucial principles behind looking after yourself. There won't be many of these.

**Important goals** are those which should be seen as a priority, fuelling the overall Essential goal, but they can also be overlooked if absolutely necessary.

**Optional goals** are "nice to have". They can help and will make life easier but don't worry if you can't achieve them.


Examples:

· · ·

## Essential:

- Protect yourself from harm.
- Escape to safety.

## Important:

- Avoid any violence initially.
- Keep your hands up to protect your head.
- Block or avoid any attack.
- Stay on your feet.
- Neutralize or counter-attack the opponent if needed.

## Optional:

- Find Police and report the incident.
- Keep your limbs free (Avoid getting tangled up).
- Maintain distance.
- Make a lot of noise and remain confident.
- Use keys or coins for distraction.
- Keep palms open.
- Mix high and low techniques for more effect.
- Deliver powerful, effective strikes.

Note that these goals are somewhat fluid and may move between categories as priorities shift between individuals. As a simple guideline try to focus on avoidance, escape and evasion rather than thinking of just how badly you wish to beat your opponent.

You will also see that not all of these are 'hard' physical techniques. Some are more 'soft' skills aimed at improving your overall response.

. . .

**Exercise:**

Take a notebook and spend a few minutes thinking about which of these are most important to you (and consider others not listed here). If, for example, you place escaping highly (as you probably should) then establishing a basic level of fitness will be very important. If however, you know you are an excellent runner but not very strong you may wish to focus on developing striking power through drills or simple strength-building exercises.

Or perhaps you value the ability to be loud and confident but you are normally quiet and shy. You may need to learn how to switch this on.

It is beyond the scope of this book to explore every potential facet of our physical and mental ability but most people already know their own abilities and limitations.

As you work down your list look at each point and compare it against your own strengths and weaknesses. This will give you a broad blueprint for developing self-defense skills and a guide to which practical techniques will work best for you.

For further reading on self-defense priorities and a detailed breakdown of how to achieve them, check out the second title in this series; *Self-defense Made Simple* at: http://getbook.at/SelfDefense

# WHAT TO DO WHEN THINGS HAVE GONE WRONG

If the situation hasn't gone to plan or you haven't been able to escape as intended you must consider the implications; the aftermath of what just happened.

### *Injury Assessment*

When the confrontation has ended, you will need to assess for injuries before moving. Start by trying to wiggle your fingers and toes. This will help you discover any broken bones or torn muscles. Next, try to locate any sharp pains, blood, or any numb, cold, or hot areas.

Use your tongue to check for split lips or cracked teeth. Slowly go over the rest of your body, one piece at a time, to assess any injuries. Try to relax. If you do discover any injuries, then you will need a calm head to determine what actions to take next.

Turn your attention to your perceptions. Note whether your heartbeat is fast or slow. Ask yourself if you feel dizzy, or if your vision is impaired. Try to focus on objects nearby, and then others which are far away. Also, note any sensitivity to light. These kinds of observations will help determine if you have a concussion.

Next, try to find someone to help you with your injuries if you have them. If you call someone to assist you, be as specific as you can about your location and injuries. This will aid them in locating you, should you lose consciousness before you are found. Do your best to stay calm and positive. Willpower is an amazing tool in the survival game.

If you are bleeding, then try to locate the source. Use whatever you have available to press against your wound, in order to slow the bleeding. Every limb has a compression point, which can be helpful in controlling the bleeding in a badly damaged limb. If bandages are available, then apply pressure to your wound to create a seal.

Top Tip: Handkerchiefs may seem out-dated but they are excellent tools for treating cuts and folding as impromptu bandages. Consider carrying one.

If the blood soaks through a layer, apply another without removing previous ones to avoid disturbing the clotting process. It may be possible to use a plastic ID card or cellophane coated cigarette box to staunch the bleeding.

In the event that you have an object, such as a knife, lodged in your body, do not attempt to remove it. The object may be the only thing preventing you from bleeding out. Wait for medical assistance.

If you are badly injured, such as by a deep cut, broken bone, or internal bleeding, then try to stay as still as you can. Moving around could exacerbate your injuries.

In the event that you have escaped unharmed, move your attention to your clothing. The condition of your clothing may provide valuable evidence if you were assaulted. Before undressing, allow a law enforcement officer to document your appearance. In the event of a rape, this is particularly important. If you have suffered sexual assault then a Rape-Kit should also be collected by the emergency room staff before showering.

Try to determine, whether any of your wounds could have made contact with your assailant's body fluids. If that is a possibility, then you will need to be evaluated for bloodborne pathogens. These kinds of evaluations are particularly important if you have been bitten.

•   •   •

## Plan of Action

Before an altercation occurs, take the opportunity to consider what you would do if it did. Plan what you would do both during the attack, and immediately afterward. When you are in that kind of situation, it will difficult to think clearly. You might even find yourself in shock, or distracted by the adrenaline rushing through your body.

Top Tip: Save a bullet-pointed plan in your phone.

(Most modern phones allow for notes to be saved. By recording a few simple tips you can ensure you have a reference even if you cannot think clearly after the event)

Shock is a natural chemical reaction, which can occur in response to injuries, or stress, such as that derived from being interviewed by a police officer. It is not unusual to experience uncontrollable shaking. Some individuals will be haunted by recurring dreams for several days afterward. Rest assured that these are all healthy and natural responses. If you do not feel ready to answer questions from law enforcement, because you are not feeling well, or your thoughts are all jumbled, then you can request some time to calm down first.

## Responsibilities

When you are no longer in danger, it is time to recognize your responsibilities. If you have wounded someone then it is your responsibility to report the occurrence to the authorities. Expect to be asked numerous questions about the event. The way in which you speak and approach these questions will affect the outcome.

By following the approaches to de-escalation and passive behavior you can drastically reduce the odds that you will be seen as the offender.

The police will use your responses to gauge whether charges will be filed. This will determine whether you will be going home, or to jail and eventually prison. Being the first to contact police after an altercation will add to your credibility. This may prove invaluable should you require a legal defense in a court of law.

. . .

### Evidence

After a physical confrontation, there may be valuable evidence on your person. This will be especially important should your assailant manage to escape before the authorities arrive. This evidence should be collected and, if possible, used to obtain a conviction in the future.

DNA testing has become increasingly popular in court cases. It is worth reiterating, that in serious cases, if you have been attacked or raped, then you should not shower, wash your hands, or change your clothes before being examined. Bits of your assailant's DNA may cling to stray hairs or skin beneath your fingernails.

Once you are safe, have been examined by a medical professional, and have answered all questions asked by law enforcement, you should sit down and write your own statement. Be as detailed and accurate as possible.

Your memory can change and fade over time. It is best to capture the events as soon as possible.

It may help to begin with an outline of the big events. Then fill in all of the blanks and details between them. This will assist you not only in any legal battle but also as you begin on the path to psychological recuperation.

# PART FOUR
# STRIKING BACK

# POWERFUL AND SIMPLE SELF-DEFENSE TECHNIQUES

The following pages show OPTIONS for self-defense in a number of situations and body areas. They really are options though because there is no 100% right and wrong in most incidents, the only important thing is that you DO act.

In fact, the only wrong approach would be to do nothing.

The techniques are designed to be powerful, simple and largely intuitive so they should be easy to pick up and flow in a natural manner. You don't like them? That's fine too ... they are only a starting point to get you thinking of the right approach that works for you.

One type of defense is great for one person while it may be useless for another. Are you 6'6" but built like a stick? – Reach is your friend. Heavy-set and shorter? – You will have stability and power. Adapt these methods for your own use.

## Where is?...

*Wondering where the defense against a flying kick or Samurai Sword-wielding madman is?*

It's impossible to detail the appropriate defense and counterattack against every possible aggressor. People come in all shapes and sizes and with a huge variety of abilities. Some are drunk, high, or just plain crazy and some are none of those. Because of this, it is not worthwhile trying to figure out how to defeat every variable.

You will see there aren't hundreds of techniques listed here. This is again intentional. We aren't trying to learn some complicated system; simplicity is the key to effectiveness. Most attacks follow the same lines and so we can usually prepare for the most common threats and the direction they come from without getting bogged down in learning hundreds of methods for countering rare and unusual attacks.

It is better to be proficient at a small amount of the most useful techniques than poor at every technique.

# ABOUT THE IMAGES

They say a picture paints a thousand words and images certainly do help in understanding what movements and combinations look like.

The pictures in this guide are designed to give you an overview of what techniques look like when performed but they aren't perfect. 100% accurate representations of perfect self-defense techniques would be a fine goal, but ultimately unrealistic. Since life and especially self-defense happens in a rough, messy and imperfect way.

Including images of intricately arranged blocks and flawless martial arts stances would be a false representation of the real world.

Hence the following pictures though clear, aim to show the broad techniques applied in a realistic, if not perfect manner, all performed by a mix of people. Not all self-defense veterans with years of experience in combat arts.

You will find that the broad movements, the key points, are the most important with regards to self-defense. Keeping your hands up, protecting your head and delivering a good strike and escape all deliver better returns for your effort than spending hours obsessing over a foot position or complicated joint lock.

Additional thanks to the people who helped out with the photos for this guide, and for volunteering as self-defense subjects.

· · ·

**Note: To avoid repetition, the very first and last move in many of the techniques has not been illustrated since it is almost always the same.**

1. Any technique starts with the open-hand guarding block.
2. Any technique ends with the return to open-hand guarding block, a scan (look around) and escape, (running away).

# TECHNIQUES: THE GUARDING BLOCK

The 'guarding block' or just 'guard' is where it all starts, as far as physical self-defense goes. If you take one technique from this book, let it be this and you will already be 50% better protected than most people on the streets.

As you may have seen in the myriad martial arts out there when a scrap kicks off it is important to have our hands up protecting the most important part of our body – the head.

(Remember, the head and brain is like a light switch; the control for the rest of the body. If it gets turned off it's going to go dark. We don't want that!)

While most arts use this guard they are doing one fundamental thing wrong for a real-life street encounter. They use clenched fists.

*Traditional Fighting Guard.*

Keeping the hands up, arms in front of the chest and elbows pointing down is a solid stance protecting our face head and, if done correctly our ribs, but doing this with clenched fists has several disadvantages:

- It shows aggression.
- It shows you are prepared to fight.
- It shows you may know some martial arts or boxing skills.
- It tenses the arm.

**The right way:**

Instead, try the same position but with open palms facing the opponent.

In an almost supplicating gesture. It signals a lack of aggression which could be vital if the incident is caught on CCTV for example but it is also just as effective (if not more so) as the traditional clenched fist guard.

## Open-hand guard:

- Is a calming gesture.
- Appears non-aggressive.
- Gives away no-information about your abilities.
- Relaxed and easy to strike from.

*Open Hand Guard.*

1. Place feet a comfortable distance apart. Usually about shoulder width. Your body should be slightly turned away facing at about a three-quarter angle.
2. Elbows are pointing down to protect your sides.

3. Most Importantly – hands are open and facing the opponent in a calming gesture. One is slightly ahead of the other (The lead hand).
4. If required, pivot the hips and drive the front palm heel forward, turning the guard into a strike within a split second.

*Easily adapted into a counter-attack or push.*

# HOW TO USE YOUR UPPER BODY

The upper body is your go-to area for striking and blocking an opponent. Not because it is necessarily any better than using legs or knees but simply because it is more natural. In a tight spot when adrenaline clouds our judgment we usually fall back on our most primal instincts.

Think about it. If you look up and noticed something falling toward you what is the most natural reaction? If you answered anything except *cover your head* you are probably fooling yourself.

We instinctively use our hands as a primary defense tool in most circumstances in which we are unable to run away. Capitalize on this instinct by learning a few effective, easy techniques involving your hands, elbows, and arms.

Generating power in upper body techniques is much more closely related to core strength than that of our arms and particularly that of the hips and abdomen. The power and speed of rotation through your torso drives the movement of a limb and so if you are keen to improve your punching and general striking power then abdominal and core drills are going to be very beneficial.

Some martial arts and combat styles focus more on upper body techniques than others. Boxing, Wing Chun Kung Fu, and Muay Thai are all worth looking at if you wish to improve upper body ability. Even if you just want to practice at home, drills designed to strengthen and test the balance of the abdomen, back and chest will be beneficial.

Exercises include:

- Standard push-ups
- Push-ups with balance elements (one hand, one leg, sidestep push-ups, inchworm or tiger push-ups).
- Standard sit-ups
- Sit-ups with a one-two punch
- Sit-ups with a twist and punch to each side
- Pike sit-ups
- Plank
- Forearm plank to hands and back to forearms

- Russian Twist
- Oblique and reverse oblique crunches
- And many more

Start slow and small, aiming for just eight repetitions with good form. Once you become proficient, aim for three or four sets of ten repetitions for a great core workout and a benefit to overall fitness.

None of these require any special gym equipment and can easily be performed at home or on a floor mat but do a search online for the correct posture for each exercise if you are unsure.

Assuming you have a strong upper body and core, strikes will naturally flow with more power, but the technique is also hugely important. Next, we will take a look at one often overlooked, element of striking; how to make a proper fist.

# HOW TO MAKE A 'PROPER' FIST

Firstly, bear in mind punches, as far as self-defense goes, are limited in application. Even though it's the first technique most people think of I would suggest never striking with a punch to an opponent's head – there is too much bone and you are likely to break some fingers. Those areas are ideal targets for palm-heel strikes or elbows.

Punches are good however for soft tissue targets. The stomach, ribs, kidneys and even throat make excellent striking zones.

Most people have no problem making a fist if you ask them to, but often those without training make a couple of errors in shaping the hand for striking.

. . .

**Making a simple fist:**

1. Open the hand out wide, palm facing the ground.
2. Curl the fingers into the palm.
3. Tuck the thumb away and underneath. (Not inside!)

## Which Knuckles?

If you want to start an argument in a group of martial artists or combat students, just ask them which knuckles you should aim to punch with. Should it be the first larger two including the index and middle finger? Or should it be the lower three?

Many traditional styles like Karate advocate the first two, while a number of boxers and Kung Fu students suggest the smaller three.

There are pros and cons of both; The big two are perhaps a bit stronger, but the lower three align better with the arm. That said, ask anyone who broke their hand in training and it's usually the pinkie finger or one of the lower metacarpals that breaks.

So what is better?

Here's the thing, despite what many so-called experts will tell you, in a real-life self-defense situation, it doesn't matter which knuckles you use because you won't have time to think about it. In training or controlled circumstances you can perfect your form and deliver beautiful punches all day, but when real life throws a big, ugly drunk attacker at you, all that goes out the window.

Instead, in the spirit of a three-second defense, focus on punching only when you need to and then to soft tissue areas or sensitive spots like the nose or groin. Don't worry about your knuckles, just hit and escape.

. . .

## Keep relaxed

The most common mistake many people often also make with a fist is keeping it tense all the time. By engaging all the arms in your muscle to tighten up a fist, you not only tire out your arm but drastically slow down any technique.

Instead, try keeping the hand in a loose relaxed fist shape with little to no tension, until about two inches before the target, then quickly tighten everything up as hard as you can, aiming to strike about two to three inches through the target on the other side. After the punch, once more relax and move.

## Vertical vs. Horizontal:

After the discussion of knuckles, perhaps the next oldest debates in martial and combat arts is whether you should hold your hand vertical (Thumb on top) or horizontal/flat (Thumb to the side).

*Vertical or Stand-Fist Punch*

*Horizontal Punch*

Kung Fu and compact Chinese arts like Wing Chun traditionally favor the former but many styles like TaeKwonDo and Kickboxing go for Horizontal.

Numerous theories espouse the benefits of one way or another.

Vertical fists are said to be quicker, easier to slip through an opponent's guard and improve body, wrist and hand alignment.

Horizontal fists are thought of as longer reaching and hence more powerful on delivery.

So is there a right way and a wrong way?

Sort of.

Ultimately the best position is the one that works for you. Just as everyone has certain techniques they find easy and others they can't quite nail, you will find that one fist feels natural while the other doesn't.

You can always develop a weaker strike through repetition and practice but it's much easier to play to your strengths and use the one that feels right for you.

Most people will find their fist naturally falls to about 45 degrees when extended but if yours doesn't that is nothing to worry about.

## Find your Natural Position

One way to find your natural fist:

1. Stand completely relaxed, arms at your side.
2. Focus on something away from your body, on the other side of the room.
3. Without thinking make fists and bring your arms up straight out in front.
4. Observe whether your hands are vertical, horizontal or at some kind of tilt in the middle.

This should be the natural bodily angle for your punching fist.

# DEFENSE AGAINST A SWINGING (HAYMAKER) PUNCH

**High Block, Palm Heel**

A big swinging punch is one most commonly seen thrown by a drunk, unprepared or untrained aggressors. Luckily it is also easier to counter than many techniques.

*This combination flows straight from guarding block and intercepts any mid to high-level attack. It follows up with a devastating strike to the face and, as always, the escape.*

1. From the open hand guarding block, raise the nearest arm to intercept the attackers swing (Most untrained attackers will swing a punch). Keep the arm relaxed and bent to deflect the energy.
2. At the same time bring your rear arm straight up and

forward, hard and fast. Keep the fingers out of the way and aim to hit with the hard part (heel) of the hand.

3. Strike to whatever you can reach. Nose and jaw are the most obvious targets but throat or eyes can also work. Once contact is made push the opponent's head back.

4. As the opponent staggers bring both arms back to guard, scan around and make your escape.

# DEFENSE AGAINST A STRAIGHT PUNCH

**Straight Block, Back Fist**

This technique comes into play if an attacker uses a straight punch in a direct forward motion. This is typically rarer as it requires some knowledge of striking on their part. Straight punches cannot be blocked directly, they are too powerful, and instead, we deflect and dodge, pushing the power of the attack past us.

1. From the open hand guarding block, twist your body weight slightly to the side. Just enough to be out of the path of the strike.
2. At the same time use your forward hand to slap the attacking punch away and slightly down. (Forearm also works well). Again not too far.
3. Using the momentum from the block, bounce your forward hand back and onto the bridge of the opponent's nose. (Or the side of the head).
4. (Optional) Instead of a back-fist, use the side of your hand to make a hammer-fist strike in the same manner.
5. Return arms to guard. Hopefully, the opponent has eyes watering and/or they have a broken nose.
6. Scan around and make your escape.

# CLOSE RANGE DEFENSE

## Close-Guard, Elbow Strike

A technique focused on a close-range threat of any kind, this method employs one of the most powerful strikes available; the elbow. Once an attacker is too close for an effective punch or palm strike we guard our head and strike short and fast.

1. The open hand guarding block is pulled tighter as the opponent has created a threat by closing within our space.

2. As always one leg is slightly ahead of the other. This front leg is the same as our striking arm.

3. Cover the side of your own head and chest by bringing the hand to the side of the head (as if listening to headphones) or by keeping the rear arm near your jaw. The elbow still points down covering the chest.

4. At the same time, bring the forward elbow horizontally into the attacker's head aiming typically for the temple area (but eyes, ears or jaw works well too). Twist the body with this motion for extra impact.

5. Repeat if needed or jab the elbow hard into the area at the base of the neck, aiming for the collarbone. This often breaks easily.

6. Push the attacker away and recover into guarding-block.

7. Scan around for danger, and then run away.

# FRONT CHOKE DEFENSE

## Pluck and Kick

If an attacker grabs us with both hands, attempting a choke or strangling motion, there are a lot of different defenses available. The most effective is the most instinctive; bringing our hands up to address the choke immediately. This employs speed and reactions to defeat power and strength.

1. The attacker catches us unawares and grabs the throat from the front.
2. Bring both hands up quickly, over and inside the attacker's hands.
3. In a fast motion yank (Pluck) the hands away and down. We are not fighting with strength but speed, quickly plucking the opponent's hands away.
4. Follow up with a fast kick to the groin.
5. Scan and escape or if needed apply a palm strike or knee then escape.

# DEFENSE AGAINST A COLLAR GRAB

## Reach over and twist

An attacker grabbing our collar can seem like a scary event but they have actually just given you a great target on which to use leverage against them. Once again we employ speed and surprise to counter their strength and aggression.

1. An aggressor grabs the collar with an outstretched arm and threatening motion.
2. From the open hand guarding block, we quickly use a circular motion to reach over the top with our opposite arm and grasp their hand in ours. (Note you can use the whole hand or place a thumb on top and fingers underneath).
3. While holding their hand firmly, quickly twist your body and snap the grabbed hand across and round, bringing it toward your hip. (On the side making the grab.)
4. With the attacker twisting, and their hand now turning upside down, deliver push hard and fast into their locked out elbow.
5. This creates a lever twisting your opponent's face to the ground and giving you complete control.
6. Neutralize the attacker if needed with a kick to their face or strike to their elbow and escape.

# HOW TO USE THE LOWER BODY

**The lower body is a high reward, high-risk area when it comes to self-defense.**

Using kicks and knee strikes can be incredibly powerful and the muscles that engage are some of the strongest in the body BUT we need our legs to stay upright and so flinging your legs around like an action movie star is an extremely BAD idea.

The real benefit, however, of lower body attacks, is that they are usually unexpected. As mentioned in the upper body section, most people instinctively use their arms in a threat situation. For this very reason, a swift low kick will be much more likely to catch an opponent off guard and give you the precious distraction you need to escape.

A recommendation is to utilize a one-two combination using both upper and lower body.

First – block, intercept or dodge an opponent's attack high-up, then counter with a sharp and low kick to a sensitive area (Shin, knee, groin, etc.)

Then run.

This approach uses our natural instinct to block with our upper body followed quickly by an unexpected low section counter-attack.

### Recommendations

Many traditional styles focus heavily on kicking, including:

- Thai Kickboxing
- Savate
- Taekwondo
- Karate
- Kung Fu

While these do help you develop strength, speed, and technique in your kicks they are also usually too high and too elaborate for real street use.

For this reason, you may wish to take what you have learned in a traditional art and adapt it for more practical use, through some reality-based training.

# LUNGING ATTACK DEFENSE

## Pushing Block, Round/Side Kick to Knee

This sequence is a great defense for a lunging type attack or, as before, a straight punch. We deflect the initial strike and counter with a powerful low kick before, as always, running.

1. From the original open hand guarding block, we twist and use the momentum to palm an attack away from the direction of the body removing the initial threat.
2. Follow up by kicking hard with the front leg, low to the side of the opponent's knee area. (Lift the knee, twist the hip and strike with the laces-part of the shoe or sole)
3. The kick can be aimed successfully at any soft or sensitive target but the side of the knee is a great target. Ribs can also work in this angle.
4. Don't wait for the attacker to recover. Again, arms are up, scan around and make your escape.

# SWINGING OR HAYMAKER HIGH-PUNCH DEFENSE #2

**High Block, Low Kick**

Very similar to the *High Block, Palm Heel,* this method instead follows up with a low kick to a sensitive area. This combination of high and low makes it difficult to predict for the enemy.

1. From the open hand guarding block, raise the nearest arm to

intercept the attackers swing (Most untrained attackers will swing a punch). Keep the arm relaxed and bent to deflect the energy.

2. Follow-up with a counter at the same time by kicking hard with the rear (Opposite) leg aiming for the groin.

3. Remember a groin strike may double the attacker over – don't get head-butted as they go down.

4. Don't wait for the attacker to recover. Again, keep hands up, scan around and make your escape.

# KNEE STRIKING

ust like the elbow, the knee is a very powerful but very short-range technique best employed when you have no distance to run or perform a full-length strike.

1. With the opponent at close range and no space to escape we reach up to grab either the shoulders or head to stabilize the strike.
2. Bring the rear knee up hard and fast to the belly or chest, while bringing the opponent down at the same time.
3. After striking, push away, bring the arms up and escape.

# DEFENSE AGAINST A GROIN KICK

## Leg Twist and Kick

This one is mostly for the fellas out there. If someone goes for a big swinging kick toward the groin it only requires a small movement to make their strike ineffective. At the same time, we position ourselves to counterattack afterward.

1. From the open hand guarding block, the attacking kick comes in.
2. Turn your waist and slightly bend your front knee as you twist the leg across, creating a block with your leading leg, closing off the groin area.
3. As the front leg pivots lift it slightly and if possible deflect the enemy kick.
4. With the leading leg and knee already raised, you can step and deliver a kick to the opponent's leg. (The type of kick is less important than making it hard and fast, but side-kicks and toe/snap kicks work well).
5. As the opponent staggers, step back with your hands up, check around and escape.

# TECHNIQUES: EXTRAS

We always aim to learn the most useful techniques and that means training and gaining knowledge about the most common kinds of attacks, not necessarily every kind of attack. Most untrained attackers will fling a wild punch or go for a grab, but some common threats don't come from a direction we are facing and don't come from a punch or kick.

The following are a couple of defenses against aggression from non-linear approaches. They can also be combined with some of the previous strikes to enhance effectiveness.

## Wall Defense, Against Attack From Behind

If you ever get caught with your back to an attacker (like in a restroom) this can be an effective counter. Assuming we haven't registered the threat until we have been hit this method allows us to defend our head, get arms up guarding and counter all in one movement.

1. When facing a wall or surface we are pushed or attacked from behind.
2. Firstly, our hands come up either side of the head to stop us from hitting the wall. This also is the start of a guarding block.
3. Pivot the head and quickly look over your shoulder at the attacker, hand on the wall. This gives you a fast visual acquisition of threat but also prevents your face impacting the wall.
4. Side kick backward hard and fast, aiming for the mid-section or knee.
5. Caught off guard the enemy is doubled over or distracted. Follow up with a palm strike or shove if needed, and move around them.
6. Disengage, keep the arms up, look around and escape.

# BEAR HUG DEFENSE, ATTACK FROM BEHIND

More often targeted against women, this threat actually engages both the attacker's arms leaving us ultimately free to counter with either of our own.

There are several steps to this defense and you may find any of them are effective. Do not feel that you have to undertake all of them. Once you are free, make your escape.

1. When facing away we are grabbed from behind.
2. Snap the head back aiming to break the attacker's nose. (If they aren't smart they may be too close and get caught by this).
3. Stamp your foot down aiming to injure the attacker's toes or feet.
4. If neither of these resulted in your release, now quickly bend your legs, drop your weight and bend slightly forward thrusting the arms out in one motion. This makes it very hard for anyone to hold on to you. (Speed and sudden movement is essential for success).
5. Freeing an arm/elbow, spin in the loosened grip and reverse elbow strike your attacker on the side of the head, repeat if needed on the other side.
6. Once freed from the grip, twist yourself free, keep the arms up, scan and escape.

# SECRET TIP: THE MOST COMMON KILLER MISTAKE WHEN 'AIMING LOW'...

If you've spent any amount of time studying Self-defense systems online or in books you will notice a recurring theme that always seems to surface. When dealing with a male aggressor 'Aim Low'.

The swift kick to the groin is a staple of so many martial arts and self-protection schools that it has almost become a running joke.

*If in doubt kick him in the nuts!*

The first thing to understand is that the reason this is so popular is that when done correctly, it is an immensely effective technique. Ask any man who has suffered accidental football to the balls and he will tell you all about the mind-numbing pain and horrifying ache that suddenly overcomes us after a strike to our most sensitive of regions. Now imagine that strike is no longer accidental but a full-strength kick and we have a crippling insta-win technique to disable any potential attacker of the male persuasion.

BUT...

There is one thing 90% of systems forget in teaching this all-winning tactic. Hit someone in the nuts and they double over in pain, smashing anything in their way.

Chances are you need to be close to deliver a decent groin kick and not have it spotted from a mile off. Because of this, you will be near your enemy when you strike.

As the knee or foot goes in, he snaps forward in pain and WHACK! You've been head-butted on the nose. (As someone who has received a broken nose I do not recommend it. Blood can choke you in the throat and eyes watering makes it impossible to see properly).


**So why bother?**

So why are there so many groin kicks in this and other guides? Because it is an effective technique but needs to be combined with a proper guarding block.

If you have the hands up protecting your head, as discussed before, you have much more control over your strike. You can choose to stabilize by holding a part of the enemy, twist away if close, or block your face and head as he doubles over in pain.

This way you combine perhaps the most powerful offensive technique (The groin kick) with the best defense; (The open-hand guard).

So remember 'Aim Low'...but only if your hands are up high!

.  .  .

### The alternative?

Another highly effective alternative kick is the pushing front kick, sometimes known as a 'Teep' in Thai kickboxing circles. The principle is very similar but the Teep requires less closing on an enemy and actively gives you space after the technique. The Teep can also be delivered to the groin, thigh, knee or any location that might be sensitive.

How to deliver a pushing front kick/Teep:

- Pick the front knee up and aim the knee at your target.
- Kick out and make contact with the ball of the foot, curling the toes back.
- As you contact, rock the hips forward slightly and 'push' with your leg, shoving the attacker back.
- Don't leave the leg out. Bend the knee and bring the foot back to the floor to reset into a stable guard position.

# WEAPONS

Weapons add a whole new dimension to self-defense and are worthy of an entire book on their own. This book is mainly focused on interpersonal unarmed self-defense, not weapon attacks; however, a few simple concepts can be applied to minimize risk should an attacker utilize a weapon.

Note that we are still (and always) trying to use intuition and natural reactions when it comes to being attacked. In this way, many weapon strikes can be defended in the same way as a swinging punch.

If you are interested in using a weapon yourself it is recommended to employ it as a distraction to help you evade the situation and not to get into a fight. A thrown set of keys or ashtray tossed as a distraction is a better choice than attempting to bludgeon the attacker with them!

For further reading, see the chapters on weapons in my other title *Self-defense Made Simple*.

## Basics

### Knives:

Knives are messy and risky weapons. In most altercations, both parties will end up getting cut. If escape is not possible try to maintain a bodily distance from the blade, keeping your torso and head away from the cutting edge. This could mean kicking low to escape or blocking at a range.

## Guns:

Thankfully rarer than knives in most parts of the world, firearms are extremely dangerous and if possible you should not even attempt to disarm a potential attacker. If you must do so, first focus on moving your body out of the line of fire, then counter-attack.

Here it is CRUCIAL that you disable the opponent's ability to fire at you by twisting the weapon free of their grip or preventing their ability to shoot at all. Break their fingers, blind them, or ideally remove the weapon altogether because firearms are one of the few cases where running away does not ensure safety.

On the plus side, if someone points a gun at you, chances are they want something like your wallet or your car and as such, it's better to hand these over.

**Bats:**

With a baseball bat or swung weapon like a stick, instinct tells us to get out of range and we should, especially if we can run away but if cornered or forced to fight back, the second-best place to be against a bat attacker is up close, right next to their body.

At this distance, the bat has no power and the attacker has lost momentum. This may run counter to intuition in many circumstances but does offer an advantage against swung weapons.

# PART FIVE

# TRAINING AND GOING FORWARD

# SELF-DEFENSE CLASS CHECKLIST:

Specific self-defense classes are highly recommended to give you regular practice in learning not only the techniques of self-defense but the ability to perform under pressure.

Unfortunately, with the hundreds of martial arts, MMA and combat schools out there, it can be difficult to know if the class you are considering is going to teach you effective techniques and methods to stay safe, or simply drain your wallet.

Sometimes, even after watching a couple of sessions, it's hard to figure out if the system being taught will be effective on the street. After all, most of us try to avoid conflict in our daily life, not embrace it.

Here are four quick tips for finding a good self-defense class that works:

## 1. Simplicity
The techniques they teach and the methods for protecting yourself should be extremely simple and effective. This makes them far easier to remember and pull off under high-stress scenarios.

· · ·

## 2. Instinctive

Even if a technique is simple, if it flows against the natural way you move, it's pretty much useless. Any good class will teach methods that utilize the body's own instinctive movements.

## 3. Usability

Any techniques taught should have definite street uses and no vague concepts about practical applications. Even better is if the techniques have multiple uses.

## 4. Anything Goes

Survival is about doing what it takes to stay alive. That means anything that works is viable. Groin strikes, eye gouges. Anything. Avoid a class which bans certain techniques or forces students to adhere to certain codes of practice in life or death scenarios.

# HOW TO CREATE YOUR OWN SELF-DEFENSE DRILLS

Drills are generally a specific exercise repeated under different circumstances, over and over until perfect. While the aim of this guide is instinctive self-defense without the need for complex maneuvers, you can improve your preparedness drastically by regularly drilling the basic techniques in different situations.

Instinct is, after all, not a conscious action, and so if we practice something enough it becomes a part of who we are, rather than something we have to think about and then perform. If we are intimately familiar with say a block and strike combination, it becomes part of muscle memory. Then when it is needed in real life we just react. No thinking, just action.

Of course, this is the ultimate aim but life gets in the way with work, family and busy schedules.

If however, you have time or space, or if you are already a member of a martial arts or self-defense club, the following is a great approach to developing effective drills for any exercise.

Developing a technique:

1. Take a single technique you wish to learn. E.g. A Palm Strike.
2. Get a partner or friend to hold a focus mitt/pad and practice striking the pad using the technique from a static position ten times.
3. Next, practice the same technique on the pad but with the pad holder first moving backward (you are attacking with the strike), then forward (you are retreating with the strike) along a straight line in the gym, ten times.
4. Now do the technique with the partner on the pad but now they keep the pad down and only pop it up when they want you to strike. The pad holder also moves in a natural manner, forward, back and circularly as if in a fight.
5. Finally perform the technique moving around with the partner in many different ways, at many different distances, and with irregular timing.

Don't forget to practice on both sides of your body (left and right arms and legs) and to give your partner a go at the same exercise.

1. **Single technique.**
2. **Single technique moving forward and backward.**
3. **Single technique moving around with a partner.**

4. **Single technique moving around with irregular timing.**

Next, you can add another aspect, say the high section block and repeat the process until you have a full block and counter exercise. The aim is to gradually increase realism by changing speed, distance and how predictable the target is, all while slowly improving the skill.

## Pressure Testing

The final step is pressure testing. Now we try to get as close to a real violent encounter as possible.

In this case, the attacking partner may use a focus mitt, or simply controlled attacks, but will not let the defender know which attack is coming.

The defender can utilize any number of blocks and counter-attacks against an unknown attack or direction.

This can be stepped up by:

- Dimming or changing the lighting.
- Adding noise.
- Adding multiple attackers.
- Limiting the defender's abilities. (E.g. One hand is tied behind their back).
- Fighting from the ground or a disadvantaged position.

Start slow and practice each technique with gradually increasing pressure and unpredictability. Work with your partner or friend and develop your skills together. Most of all, try to have fun! If you enjoy learning, you are much more likely to stick at it.

# THANK YOU (AND A FREE BOOK!)

I can't stress enough that any real life or death encounter will probably not go to plan and even if you only remember a few of the techniques listed here, you will have a great advantage. Trust your instinct and never be afraid to run. If you can't run then try to calm the situation, if the attacker wants your money hand it over – it's only money.

It's only after all of this and if you still genuinely fear for your safety that you should start to think about blocks and counter-attacks. They are always a last resort.

Luckily, violent events are still rare, so while preparation is great, you can rest assured that with a bit of awareness and preparation you can avoid a dangerous scenario altogether.

**Thank you.**

So thank you for reading this guide. I work hard to create useful and easy to follow guides for martial arts, fitness, and self-defense. I hope you never have to use it!

Given that you now have a better understanding of self-defense, please help others and give this book a quick positive review if you found it useful or learned something new.

Reviews take only a few seconds and make a world of difference to authors and other readers alike. I aim to read each one personally, so thank you in advance.

Finally, for a **COMPLETELY FREE** guide to developing explosive power through Plyometric skills, check out my site at:
   **www.BlackBeltFit.com**

Thanks again and stay safe.

*- Phil Pierce*

# HOW TO MEDITATE IN JUST 2 MINUTES: EASY MEDITATION FOR BEGINNERS AND EXPERTS ALIKE

http://getbook.at/HowtoMeditate

**Given, Meditation can be an incredibly powerful tool in improving both physical and mental health, focus and relaxation but most people think it takes a long time to see results. The truth is it doesn't!**

With this easy-to-use book, you can quickly learn how to achieve these incredible benefits in just 2 minutes a day...

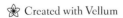